T0098407

EBURY PRESS

A BIRD ON MY WINDOWSILL

Born in Baramulla, Kashmir, Manav Kaul has been an integral part of the film world, acting, directing and writing for the past twenty years. With each of his new plays, Manav has made people sit up and take notice, and he has created an equally valuable body of work as a writer. His books *Theek Tumhare Peeche* (Right Behind You) and *Prem Kabootar* (Love Pigeon) have been dominating the Nielsen bestseller list.

Celebrating 35 Years of
Penguin Random House India

ALSO BY THE AUTHOR

Rooh

a bird on my windowsill

manav kaul

translated by
nandini kumar nickerson

EBURY
PRESS

An imprint of Penguin Random House

EBURY PRESS

USA | Canada | UK | Ireland | Australia
New Zealand | India | South Africa | China | Singapore

Ebury Press is part of the Penguin Random House group of companies
whose addresses can be found at global.penguinrandomhouse.com

Published by Penguin Random House India Pvt. Ltd
4th Floor, Capital Tower 1, MG Road,
Gurugram 122 002, Haryana, India

First published in Ebury Press by Penguin Random House India 2023

Copyright © Manav Kaul 2023
Translation copyright © Nandini Kumar Nickerson 2023

All rights reserved

10 9 8 7 6 5 4 3 2 1

The views and opinions expressed in this book are the author's own and the
facts are as reported by them which have been verified to the extent possible,
and the publishers are not in any way liable for the same.

ISBN 9780143464648

Typeset in Adobe Garamond Pro by Manipal Technologies Limited, Manipal

This book is sold subject to the condition that it shall not, by way of trade or
otherwise, be lent, resold, hired out, or otherwise circulated without the
publisher's prior consent in any form of binding or cover other than that in
which it is published and without a similar condition including this condition
being imposed on the subsequent purchaser.

www.penguin.co.in

Have you ever looked at yourself while reading?
I've written the image for you . . .

Preface

As you entered my being . . .

A long time ago, I knew of a boy who dreamed about painting. He wanted to draw himself as a bird but every time he tried, he ended up drawing a kite. Then, he would stop. He would then slowly draw the string attached to the kite flying free in the sky. Eventually, he would think that somebody was holding the string. This thought held him back from finishing his drawing. He would rip the picture and start all over again. He never drew the man who possibly held the string in his hands. And he kept on tearing one painting after the other. The word compromise never entered his mind. And then after a long time, in one of his attempts, the string snapped and finally he saw that his painting was finished. He connected the breaking with letting go and in this letting go was a freedom akin to death. In every art form, moving from difficult to easy is a normal process. I find that my writing is close to that process.

. . .

I dream a lot. When I wake up in the morning, some of these dreams are still with me, while the rest disappear with the darkness of the night. Those that are remembered have a strange voice when repeated in the morning. This is not my voice. It's his voice that tells me these stories. I always ask, 'The dreams that I forgot, did I really dream them?' I ask such questions during long travels or prolonged silences. The voice replies, 'I remember a few faded pictures of those dreams. Would you like to listen to them?' We both know that it is a lie. We don't know anything, and he knows how much I adore the thick mist of the mountains. There is so much more in not seeing than it is in clarity. How much better it is to stay quiet than to talk incessantly. We pick a spot where there is pleasure in just sitting and he starts recounting the dream.

Are the things that are forgotten not lived as well?

My mother tells me many stories from my childhood. She remembers everything; narrates these stories as if they happened yesterday. I listen to all these accounts with great interest. For a long time, we sense love in these stories. She finds me through these tales. I don't remember myself in her stories, but I do remember the spaces as if I was there last night. The cracks of the walls, the damp windows in the rain, the smell of tempered dal from next door and the kite tangled up in the wires in the neighbourhood—I can taste everything. But the people are missing from these spaces. Even I'm absent. There's a voice that is not mine. This voice says I will find Mohan at the end of this road, and I begin to see Mohan, even when he never existed. All the places stuck to my body pull Mohan from the lost dreams and bring him to me. Whereas the lost dreams were never there. And then, I pick up my pen and paper. I write to Mohan, who is standing at the end of the road, and he talks about the kite tangled up in wires in the neighbourhood.

For some time, it seemed as if I could not touch that which was actually there. I have been trying to gather the lies that exist in everything. I am unable to live with things as they really are. I was seeing people and talking to those who were never there.

I was trying to run away from the man who wrote. After a considerable contemplation, I bid farewell to him—his voice wouldn't let me be alone ever. I stopped writing. I wrote nothing for almost three years. During this time, the man would come and sit by my side sometimes, especially when I was travelling. I would ignore him and leave. On long travels I would hear his footsteps, but I was trying to convince myself that I wanted to stay away from these lies. While all this was happening, I had my phone with me, which I used to take pictures with. I would look around like a child, making sure that the man wasn't watching, and write down exactly what I was feeling in that moment. That which I can touch, I would register. I would post these notes with the pictures on Instagram. As if I had left a message in space. I think I was trying to search for this kind of writing for a long time—that's neither a poem nor a story. It is just a picture of the thickness of the time when a kite was flying away without a string.

This book contains travels, the free solitude while writing plays and stories and talks about silence. There are posts from my Instagram and has anecdotes about different stages of writing. It was like a dam that had stored the water for many years. I let it break loose in this book.

I have changed. I am not the person you once knew. Somehow, I am the same, but the dirt road we walked on has been paved. Everything green has turned grey. Afraid of falling, I have started growing roots. But the places we used to meet remain the same. Whenever I walk through their cool shade, I think of you.

Have you been to Prague? If you do go, don't forget to visit Kafka's grave. You will find a deep stillness there—the type that is left behind in bed after a long night's slumber. There are no dreams there, only cold silence. Listen to that silence; please leave behind something that once was dear to you.

They say things left behind tend to grow roots.

If you say everything will change one day, I will believe it. But then, please tell me that the sky will still stay blue and the clouds will sometimes randomly show us the faces of all the people we thought were gone forever. Will you be able to say that every loss will turn into a gain?

In the moments of sadness, when everything is going wrong and I am very close to giving up, will you wake me up with your gentle touch?

Why can't we tell those we love that we never want to lose them until we do?

If we are temporary, then only you are life. Will you not return before our clock stops ticking?

Is this the end? Have you gone too far? Listen, stop somewhere but don't say, 'I'm tired' . . . just say you are looking for shade in this harsh sun. And here I am, stuck in that part of the story where the sunlight scatters inside the empty house and I have a broom. As you sit under the shadow of a giant banyan tree, I will tell you how I swept the sunlight away. You will laugh. But that is not how our story ends. It will finally rest next to a shrine under the banyan tree.

So, instead of looking for shade, find that shrine. And if you do, there you will find shade, the banyan and the end of our tale, lying by itself.

Your body
is a sacred place
that hides these twelve black dots,
they're disappearing from my memory
with the time that is slipping away.
Fruitlessly
I try to hold on.
But every struggle to hang on to you
ends up in a bitter song.

The year is ending now
Eleven months have passed.
Gone are the eleven dots I knew.
Gone are your memories from my heart.
But one memory still haunts me.
When I saw the last black dot.
It glimmered on your neck that day.
It looked at me
from under your scarf.

Now I don't try to hold on.
My grip has given way.

I have few memories of you.
Honestly, I don't remember you at all.
Time is easy on me.
A year flies by in minutes.
But that twelfth star looking at me that day
has decided to revisit all the time.
And while all the months gently leave,
December always clings on firmly.

She was happy as they finally stepped out of the bazaar. As she felt closer to the boy, the stars seemed to go further away. The noise from the crowded streets was still between them. How easy it was to drown in it, she thought. She had thought it would be impossible to get rid of it.

But right now, she was happy. So happy that her body shivered.

The boy said, 'How long will this happiness last? Can it keep us warm when the nights turn cold—when we are shivering?'

She grew silent. What about being here, right now? He had not noticed her shivering. Maybe the boy was still in the bazaar. Fear ran through her body, but she smiled. He was not with her; he was still clutching on to what she'd left behind. And she stopped shivering.

'Let's gather some firewood,' she finally said.

'But why?' the boy asked.

'I want to burn something,' she looked up to the sky. The stars had inched much closer to her now.

After this, they both saw each other slowly dying in the flames. As the burning fire started singeing them, they turned around and walked far away from each other.

Many years later when they returned with the water of their restlessness to douse the flaming ashes, they couldn't meet each other's eyes. It's easy to let go of what is dead and gone but what of those bones that are still lying warm in the ashes?

. . .

The thing was that she was on one side of the door, and I was on the other. We both were dreamers and could not dream of each other by staying together. So, we decided to walk away, so far away that we would forget each other. Then we could only see each other in our dreams. Whenever she took my name, I felt her fragrance dance around me. Her memory enveloped me and I would start dancing. I believed I was going mad. But what is this thing called belief anyway? Was this the beginning of a dream or the ending of one? There she was, on the other side of the door. If I opened the door, it would mean the end of the story. If I let her enter, it would mean the beginning of a lie.

Deodar trees talk if you're willing to listen. I walked in, and the jungle moaned, caressing the tired, worn-out day. I looked at a tree far away and caught a glimpse. There you were. I felt a sudden urge to tell you, grab a paper and write about it, make a mad dash to post it and somehow make you understand that I saw you under a giant deodar. But could I muster up the courage to draw something as beautiful as I had seen? Could I even dare? My words started giving way; they lost gravity. I realized my visions are pure only till this jungle surrounds them. For if I let them out, they will be just as helpless as a wild beast in the city.

I wanted to write your name. But instead, I wrote 'hope'. Then, I started looking for you. I had a vision of you inside me. I said softly, 'Hope'. No, I did not say it but read what I had written.

I saw you coming towards me in an earthy dress. As you neared, I saw giant sunflowers emerge on the dress—some wilted, others blooming. The whole landscape seemed yellowish. Your arrival was the departure of many things. You were running. You wanted to fly, but you seemed stuck in the ground. I said, 'Butterfly', and you came closer.

'Where were you?' I asked.

'I was looking for water,' you wiped the sweat off your brow.

'Water?'

'Yes, water.'

'Where is it then?'

'I drank it,' you said and simply started walking again.

I wondered if she had any idea that I had been waiting for her. So, I started walking behind her. Then I said, 'Gentle', and she stopped. I was thirsty too. But I didn't have the heart to tell her that; instead, I asked, 'Where are you going?'

'To the mountains,' she replied.

And I could see the end of the desert. And from its edges was the expanse of the mountains.

'So why didn't you come here to look for water?'

'It's a different direction.'

'Yes, but if you were walking, why didn't you come here?'

'It is a different direction.'

I had never changed directions. I only had one direction, and I had to walk in that direction. Whatever I found in that direction, I collected. How can thirst and water be in two different directions? And why? I could never understand this. What does thirst have to do with the direction of the desert? You were standing silently in front of me. I was thirsty. My throat was parched. My questions were sharp around the edges. So, I remained silent. In her eyes was her need to hear that one word from me.

It's hard to ask a question and draw meaning simultaneously. So, I said, 'Mountains.' An empty road appeared with a lone tree—deodar.

There were no rules between us.
Only space.
Expansive. Encompassing. Space.
It drew in everything that went on in our lives.
The questions, fears, etc.
So, we walked in bliss. And envied what we did.
We lived. Yes, that's what we did.
We stretched our hands out to touch the light.
We tried.
Then desires grew. The space too.
We were the last ones to disappear in it.
I gave her an aspect of my life.
She gave me her picture.
Now, when my hands go out to touch the light,
it's her fragrance they find.

I've tried to write 'love'. Measure and put it into words so that it becomes precisely love. But whenever I am about to do it, I miss it by a sentence. Just as I'm about to finish, I get confused. I always feel that that one last sentence that would've justified everything eludes me as if waiting for someone. Each time! My words hold hands and start looking like love. But that final sentence runs and hides. I don't like writing words that are like love. No, I want to write love. So, I stopped writing and started thinking about everything I'd written before. In one sense it's all like love, but it's not love. Does that one sentence even exist? Or would it never settle down in a form or sound? Or perhaps it stands at my doorstep, waiting for someone to arrive . . .

Are you still living there? The flash of light that I saw; that glimmer at the end of a long dark tunnel, was that you? My mother used to say that another name for light is hope. So, I began calling you that. I still dwell in the darkness where I can't make anything out. I can only see myself when you glimmer. So, whatever colour you give out, I begin to look like it. Last time, you were red—deep, dark red. Now the blue sky is visible, are you still there? I am looking at white clouds in the sky. Are you the eagle that's just come out from the clouds? I have hope, I have light, your eyes are bright red and my sky blue.

I turned away the moment I was about to see her. When I looked back, she had left. Now, I look around and hope to see her at every turn. Familiar faces greet me, but there is no one like her. Maybe I had never seen her, and perhaps I never will. Perhaps I like turning around. The hope of seeing her is nothing but an excuse.

They had met briefly. About to leave for their respective countries, they looked at each other. His flight had been announced. He had picked up his bags. They were both smiling. It was too early for them to ask anything from the other. He hesitated, 'Can I write you a letter?'

'Last night I sneakily put my address in your bag.' The boy looked down, embarrassed that he had asked. The girl averted her gaze—pretending to check on her flight. They had spent very little time together, but it seemed as if they had started reading a story together, and before they knew it, the story had grown interesting. He took out his key ring and handed it to her; she did the same.

And then they both went their own way. The more they looked back at each other, the more they felt their eyes swell with tears.

For a long time, the woman kept waiting for his letters, knowing fully well that she had never sneaked in her address in his bag.

It was August.

We walked on dark roads, lighted cigarettes and smoked away our indecisions. The future did not seem so scary in the haze of the smoke. You said that when we have money we will go to a big hotel and order a nice dinner. And then we would think about everything we would eat that day. That August, we were so hungry and so content.

These days, I eat very little and keep fit. Honestly, I think about calling you up and asking if we could talk about the day when we'll go to the lovely hotel and order a nice dinner.

But I just heard you stopped smoking . . . *arrey!*

Whenever she looked for newness, she thought that novelty lies in things she didn't know yet. Like, she didn't know the things that she wanted. Or maybe she wanted them because she didn't know what they were. To wander alone, get stuck in places, stand at a crossroads, smile in situations that made her wonder deeply, write in solitude and speak about the silence in songs . . . were all her ways to find the new. Will she ever find it? Maybe if she looks under the deodar, banyan or peepul tree?

You have taught me to love. I always say 'fragrance' before I say your name. It's not the word but the feeling because you change every season. You are never completely rain. And when lightning strikes, you are the image in that glimmer. To see you is just a wish to see you. It doesn't need to be you. I understand you from the fragrance that constantly changes. That is the reason why I take a deep breath before I utter your name.

I am trying to wash you off my clothes. I am struggling to get rid of the memories, but the water that contained them refuses to squeeze itself out. I could dry off some clothes, but it turned out that even they didn't let go of your fragrance. They are stubborn! They make me angry, and I decide to wear new clothes. But then I don't feel like myself in them. I get tired and pick up the old ones again. They don't complain. They cling to my skin as quickly as you held me in your arms.

So, I've decided to put the new and old clothes in the bucket now with the hope that their colours rub off on one another . . . so that I seem familiar among the new and estranged among the known.

'Do things in the past stop existing?' The girl asked him as he looked outside the café. There was a rush of cars on the road, and he was thinking of someone else. The girl wanted to ask him again, but she began laughing instead.

'Why are you laughing?' the boy asked.

"Actually, nothing really ends. It just stays with one of the two people. As if the one who dies becomes free, but the one left behind carries all the moments they have lived,' she started laughing again.

'I don't understand!' The boy was looking at her in bewilderment.

'You will not understand because you are the one who has died.' She said smiling, opened the door of the cafe and left.

People tell me that I've started to look exactly like you. This had made me stand in front of the mirror and look at myself for long . . . a question occurred to me: do I look the way you are right now or the way you looked when we were together? This thought starts to bother me, and I step out to look for you. A long time passes till I see you again. I stare at you, shocked. 'Rickety' is the way you looked. I felt very old that day.

Many years have passed by, haven't they? In thinking that things will be okay one day. But that day never comes. There is only a pain that's left, and you feel it the day when you see yourself getting old, not in the mirror but reflected through someone else—for the first time!

I had many complaints with you. I would collect all my complaints before our meetings. Carefully, I stacked them up like a house of cards, hid behind them and waited for you.

'You always come late,' I decided not to use this joker card today. Instead, I just kept it in my hands. As time passed and you were nowhere to be seen, I grew angry—kept twirling the joker between my fingers. Maybe I should use this card, I thought. It's hard to when one is angry, and I didn't know when you arrived and took the seat right opposite me. I forgot my complaints, and the house of cards collapsed.

Suddenly I saw what was in your hands. A card. 'Why do you always come so early?' I showed her my watch and she showed me her watch. You were late by mine, but on time according to yours. We started smiling.

Everything seemed new when we met. There were coffee, tales and conversations. Before we knew it, we began to smell like books.

We have often stood at a crossroads, held our breath and wondered where to head next. Sometimes, it feels right that we have crossed those intersections. At least we have left behind the useless questions like 'what will you do with your life?' These fatal dilemmas made us pave the dirt road that once led us to our hearts. But we never forgot that these roads led to her house. Now, any road that looks familiar makes everything stop. It's not exactly her that you remember, but the shop where you would stop to see her or the kid whom you begged to deliver the letter or maybe the sweeper who told her brother about you or the fragrance that rises from the ground when she walked by.

'A cage went in search of a bird . . .'

While searching for Kafka's home, I could hear its musical notes from far away. I wondered if I should ask someone, 'Where did Kafka live?' But I felt that he was near me. That he will appear out of nowhere and ask, 'Did you write what you wanted to?'

So, I'll show him my long process of metamorphosing into an insect. I had been listening to him for so many years! I'll tell him that I had been lost. *I lost my bearing in my eagerness to meet you.* I will stand in front of him—just waiting until he says something beyond what words could mean. Where there will be musical notes and not words. I will watch him change again in those notes. Will I see him here?

Suddenly, I was standing in front of the place where Kafka used to live. It didn't take me too long to recognize it. This house had been my laptop's screen saver for many years. But Kafka was not there. I went inside the little door and stepped out. I went in again, but I couldn't touch him. It's strange how none of us can be found where we were last seen. We have been changing places. It's like we don't live in the whole house but in a part that we are most comfortable in. It's perhaps a corner that makes us feel safe and happy. In which corner of Prague does Kafka live then? I don't know, but I can hear him.

I went to Café Montmartre and Café Louvre looking for him, drinking endless cups of coffee. It's said he visited them often. Amid beer, wine and cigarette smoke, I searched on the roads of Prague . . . I tried but failed to catch him. Prague, for me, is Kafka, and yet why do I want to hear him somewhere else? Would he know I read his works in my tiny, rented apartment, during the most challenging times of my life? I understood what the word 'difficult' really meant. I am thinking about Nirmal Verma's *Ve Din* in Prague. But right now, all I wanted was solitude.

So I walked out of the city into the cemetery with Kafka's grave. In the wilderness, amidst many graves, I found it. His grave. I stood there in silence. Then slowly, my legs gave away, and I got down on my knees and closed my eyes. I was there for a long time, waiting to hear his voice. But he didn't speak. When I opened my eyes again, I noticed a hairpin. A girl had left it on the grave. Ah! There is such a beautiful story hidden here. I started smiling. I sensed Kafka is in his writing. 'All I am is literature, and I am not able or willing to be anything else.'

. . .

You are stepping out of your language and stepping into a foreign tongue.

2010–11: I was included in the Lincoln Centre's director's lab. Whenever I'm in New York, my feet automatically take me to the Lincoln Centre's building. Last time, when I was bidding goodbye to my American friend Mark, he wondered if we will ever experience this blissful time, meet these beautiful people again.

'I don't know,' I had replied. 'Do you ever go back to reading the same beautiful book again?'

Now, I've forgotten most of their names, and perhaps soon enough, the faces will fade away, too. A few years later I might remember the towns but forget the streets. Remember the words but forget who said them. Remember what I lost but forget what I found . . . I don't know. Every journey affects our subconscious in some manner and shows up in ways we cannot foretell. I thought all of this and sat at the café, where I had spent many empty nights, and while sipping coffee I called up Mark. When I heard his voice on the other end of the line, I said, 'Mark, we do go back to some beautiful, good books and read them again and again because every time we read them, we find something new, and that brings us closer to ourselves. Let's have a beer, friend' Mark laughed for a long time after I'd finished.

My house got burned easily; no flames shall touch you.
Someone has bought this tongue; this pen is someone's slave.

It was 1984 or '86 when they burned his house down. On being asked who these people were, the famous *shayar* (poet) Bashir Badr said that they were neither Hindus nor Muslims. It was a mob, and a mob doesn't have a religion. But the pain of having his house burnt down was playing somewhere in his subconscious. Twenty-five years later, he was diagnosed with depression and began medication. Its side-effect was that this great poet stopped writing poetry. I attended one of his *mushairas* (poetry sessions) in my youth. He was visiting Hoshangabad. It was late in the night and we were sitting in a tiny club. Every time he recited a couplet, he said, 'This is the last one', but then someone would say, 'One more,' and he politely acceded. The mushaira went on till morning, and I prayed that he would never stop. After all these years, I found myself sitting in front of him. It felt strange. I had the urge to hug him.

His memory had faded. When someone read him his poem, he smiled. Bashir sahab's wife says that, for fifty-six years, he spent all his nights at the mushairas and his daytime

27

sleeping. The scene is similar now; he stays awake during the night and sleeps during the daytime. Sadly, it's the poems that are gone.

> He, who is extremely benevolent, may he grant me this
> If I wish to forget you, may my wish not be granted.

An infinite number of people are a fan of this she'r!

. . .

Some places become dearer while travelling. When you leave them, pain echoes from deep inside. There is a ripple effect. The moment a wave settles down and you feel calm, a thought swells—it is a ripple effect. To see that city on the last day, the narrow alleys come alive and give in to the main roads. Sometimes, I feel that the lines of my hands have spread across the city and sometimes it feels likes the whole town is empty, and I'm floating across it like a ghost. Then there are faces—plenty of beautiful faces, countless birds, giant green trees and spread across the whole city are conversations over tea or coffee . . .

In the end, we leave with 'I'll return soon'. But can we return to the same place ever again? In the cities, which are constantly getting younger, there are fewer spaces to grow old. How hard it is to leave a place! And the real question is, can we leave anything?

Whenever I find myself in a lovely place, I stop and sense what is happening inside of me. I have always been curious about this. I look at everything in silence and then muster the courage to like it all and make myself believe that I do. But suddenly, I start laughing. Why do things seem beautiful when we think about them as the past? Is the present only helpful in collecting memories? Can we only find happiness by looking at the past?

When I was young and travelled a lot, I used to think about this. I was yearning to give meaning to everything and travelling in search of those meanings. I never found the answers. Now the rhythm of my journeys has changed. I still get enchanted by beautiful things but don't become numb now. I enter it and go silently inside. Finding an answer or discovering a meaning doesn't bother me anymore. I let myself go, and I become that beautiful place.

Last night I was travelling to the Krabi islands from Bangkok. The train journey was beautiful. It reminded me of a ride from Prague to Bratislava. But this one seemed freer, probably because the dining car windows were open. The sweet-smelling fresh air filled the compartment. I smoked and drank tea there most of the day and then I was the first one to order chai early in the morning. Journeys have a strange effect on you. They are not easy at all. Your body starts to feel like an old building and your back like its old, crumbling walls. Like they are peeling off. And things that seemed very important in our everyday life just fall off, making us lighter. You stand against these walls; your sweat makes shapes on them. You start to create meaning out of these shapes. But as soon as you lift your hand to touch them, they disappear. Journeys are complex and wonderful at the same time. Most importantly, they keep us away from all the mundane stuff that keeps us busy, and we call that life.

When in the evening I start to take a walk, I feel butterflies in my stomach, 'Where should I go today?' This is what I think every day. What should I do today? Cohen was right when he said, 'The older I get, the surer I am that I'm not running the show.'

When somebody asks me, 'Where are you going?' I often say, 'Just like that'. And it is right in a way. All my long journeys have started just like that. Whenever I'm lost in the jungle, I feel a strange sensation in my stomach—content that I am lost. I know that I will find my way, but I am also aware that I will not be the same person who got lost. I'll be different. Whenever I look in the mirror, I wonder, 'Who is the one looking in the mirror and who is the one looking back?'

Many pictures flash before my eyes whenever I walk on Bhopal's streets. Stop number 3, Prakash Taran Pushkar, Hostel, New Market, T.T. Nagar, then Kala Parishad, Ravindra Bhavan, the lake and in the end, Bharat Bhavan—the place where I had taken my first step on the stage and began my life as an actor. Whenever I meet people from that time, they tell me stories. I don't remember being in those stories. I asked them if I was there, and they said yes. They laugh and I lie that yes, I remember. Although I don't remember being that person, I know he would have been with them at that time. I can never relate to the person in the stories and the person who lived them. It feels as if I don't know who went through all that and who is living it now.

Someone tiptoed and whispered in my ear, 'It's a foggy day'. I jumped out of my bed and was soon walking on the streets of Delhi. The morning seemed like a wet painting. As if a painter had just slathered thick, white paint on the canvas and was waiting for it to take form. These half-made things give rise to so much imagination! Beautiful moments start swimming in this blankness. The things close by became more apparent, and those far away got blurry. Behind the chirping of the birds, I heard the clinking of teacups. I followed the sound and ended up in a small chai shop. And it was then that I realized where this foggy morning was oozing out from.

Whenever an old banyan starts a tale with 'long time ago', it feels as if I'm lying down under that tree in the afternoon, dreaming about my ancestors. They were terrific people. I realize this while walking through an old building, touching its ancient walls and feeling as if I'm trying to feel those that have passed by this way. My hands touch what they had felt, and my feet walk the same narrow alleys they had passed through. The silence holds secrets if you stay still enough to listen. If you close your eyes and let the silence speak, you can hear your ancestors. You can dream like they did, sleeping on a cot under the old peepul tree. From their time to ours, what travelled are the memories of not what we gathered but what we left behind.

Spain. I had lived in many hostels before I finally reached Valencia. I thought about staying here for some time, taking in the beauty of this town. Since I was searching for an ending for the play, *Chuhal*, I always carried a little notepad with me. I was sitting in a café one day, tearing everything I'd written down when I felt someone watching me. I looked across the table and met an old woman's gaze. There is something special that happens when you travel alone. Everything becomes so still that even a little flutter shakes you to the core. The astonishment in her eyes moved me. I decided to chase it. I gazed back. In such instances—exclusively during my travels—I don't turn away, I keep trailing that astonished look as if there is something hidden there. I felt she could see a part of me that I didn't know until now. I started finding answers to the question I didn't think I had.

The old woman disappeared after a while. I was staring at the blank page in front of me. The end of the play, *Chuhal*, had started taking shape.

I stayed in every city in Spain for two to three days. I met some very fascinating people in the hostel. We all moved on to our travels after a while. It was comforting to know you are not the only mad traveller. There are many people who are enjoying travelling without an aim. I met such a group in Granada, and we decided to see a flamenco performance on a hilltop. Although the prospect wasn't exciting for me, I accompanied my new friends. When the show started, and the performers joined one by one, I sensed their emotions. The atmosphere grew thick with feelings. The same kind of heaviness I experience when I write. Suddenly, my Spanish friend put her hand on my shoulder and asked, 'Are you okay?' I nodded and then suddenly realized my cheeks were wet. I was crying and I had no idea.

After the performance ended, we went to a pub and drank wine. Everybody was talking about the dance. I couldn't say a lot except that it was fun.

I left the city the next day, but something had changed within me, and I could not pin it down. What was it that could be seen from outside but was still not clear to me? When I reached Córdoba, a violin player was performing on the street. I stood there for some time, but that thing inside me didn't go away. I felt moved. So, I ran from the music until I couldn't hear it anymore. Finally, I stopped at a junction and saw a church right across the street. I decided to enter. Inside, a statue of Jesus Christ hung on the cross. The building was silent, and I felt a deep sense of calm enveloping me. Then, I saw an old-looking confession box hiding in a corner as if it had been lying since the time of Jesus. I could not contain my curiosity and went and sat inside. Before long, a priest came in and sat on the other side of the net. He said something in Spanish and although I couldn't understand, I didn't want to let this chance go. So, I apologized in English and then I don't know why, but I began to pour my heart out, and the words came out in Hindi. I talked about everything; the flamenco, that thing inside me and what I was feeling at that moment. The priest kept sitting there. When I finished, he looked at me and nodded.

The remains of the past can surprise us. Is *that* who we were? But somewhere, we are still the same people. While we were creating a new world, we were ending another. The world that is ending reminds us that violence always leads to destruction. And yet, we are ready to make the same mistakes again. How often will we keep repeating the same mistakes?

These ruins that are left, someone has preserved them— someone trying to tell us that underneath the colours, we are all just humans. And to kill another inevitably leads to our death.

When I was young, my village was my world. I would often run away from school and sit with Raju and Salim at the railway station to drink cheap tea and look at the end of the train tracks where all trains disappeared and came into existence again. That place was the end of the world for us. We had a lot of stories about the place beyond it. We thought that these trains must be travelling up to the boundaries of the world during the night. How could the world be any bigger than that?

Today when I have been roaming around Europe, I thought about calling Raju and Salim. I wanted to tell them that it is magical here as if it's another planet; the language, food, history, everything is different here. I was in a tiny village called James in Austria waiting for my train. I wondered if this hamlet had its Salim and Raju. Who would've thought the same way? Would they have known about our village too? It is strange to talk about it, but this village and mine have existed together in time. An altogether different world was living simultaneously with ours, and we had no clue about it.

As my train arrived and I settled into my seat, I saw two boys walking into the building. They were not there to catch a train. But in a way, they looked familiar. One of them had curly hair, and the other, a moustache. They were laughing hysterically while taking out coffee from a machine. Just like Raju and Salim. One of them saw me, and I had a sudden urge to shout out, 'I am your third friend from the other side of the world!'

The train started picking up speed. And with them, I saw my childhood village vanish into a place where things disappear and then never come back into existence again.

I saw a large herd of elephants in Sri Lanka today. A variety of animals spread across the prairie. It is the last day of the year, and my mind wonders, 'How old is the earth?' How long did it take for the Milky Way to reach 2017? It would be foolish to ask the stars their age, wouldn't it? Because they say many stars in the night sky are already dead. It's only their light that is travelling to us. The mountains don't seem like they have come from somewhere. They have always been here. They were here right from the beginning. At least that's what it seems like. But when did it all begin? Like the ebb and flow of the ocean are always present and yet moving, all these trees and animals are complete in themselves. Then a thought worried me—do they know that 2016 is ending? Should I tell these beautiful elephants that they are entering a new year? That time is passing by us so quickly?

My thoughts make me feel small. It will be a long time until we all become animals once again.

I spent the whole day walking around Chayal (Himachal Pradesh) today. I saw life slowly crawling in small spaces and on the faces of older people. Young people don't hold my attention in places like these. The small town Chayal comes to an end within a few paces. I would take the narrow dirt roads then. I stop and watch older women working busily in their tiny houses. In this village surrounded by deodars, there is a strange sort of silence. Suddenly the fog descended, and just as suddenly, it begins to rain. The few people who were roaming about also retreated. I was alone again. As I waded through the mist, it felt like I was swimming across an old, submerged civilization. The thought made me smile.

The mountains remained still while the fog danced as it rose through the bushes. Our mind looks for stability in all these. It takes time for a city person to come to a mountain finally. You can be here, and yet take a long time to arrive. It takes patience and commitment before the layers of the city start peeling off. Then, finally, it takes time to get comfortable with the silence of one's existence.

Mountains do this to me. Chayal in this fog reminds me of Kashmir. The houses around pull out memories. If not from this life, then probably from some other. But I know that I've lived here; I've seen this deodar tree grow tall in front of my eyes; I painted these windows blue and kissed you at the doorstep when our love was new. I have loved someone with all my heart here. I have waited. I have longed. I have lived.

I take comfort in knowing that these houses will keep my memories safe long after I've forgotten them.

The mountains echo all your life back to you. While a stranger's pain touches you deeply, your brooding keeps you up at night. While it's tempting to give your worries to the forests, the narrow roads make it hard to run away. The good part, however, is that the mountains forgive a sincere heart. If you are patient enough, they are patient with all your mistakes. And thus, there is no hardship when you climb them and no shame when you tumble down.

I felt like going uphill in the morning. So, I started walking in that direction. The forest sprawled on the entire hill; only a little space remained for a tiny chai shop. I reached the top in the afternoon and looked at the town below me and the sky beyond. I lay down on the grass—hunger, thirst and exhaustion. But what I could see was beautiful. I heard the pitter-patter; it had begun to rain. Running for shelter meant walking down; I decided to stay. The clouds had been ripped apart by the sun rays at a distance. A golden light was pouring from the sky. This brightness afar soothed the darkness that was nearer. The sky, although always there, looks new every day. I closed my eyes and lay down. I wanted to let this light and dark soak me. I wanted all of it, without any conversation, without any desire.

When I opened my eyes again, the rain had stopped. The dark clouds had given way to sunlight. The sky was blue again. 'What time is it?' I asked her as if she was there with me.

Mountains during the rain—how dramatic! People here say it is off-season, but I feel this is actually the time—the time to come to the mountains. The rainy season in the mountains has a certain romance, the drama of youth. Winters are like old age and summers are like the mistakes we make just before growing up, which we want to wash away with the rain. But rain doesn't wash away anything and come winters, we curse ourselves. Wish we had made some more mistakes in our summers.

Whenever I'm in Manali, I try to visit the old town and walk towards the hills beyond it. Only this time, I found a tiny chai shop nestled between these hills. I'd never seen it before. By before, I mean on my last visit, three years ago. The sight made me happy. So, I went in and took a seat. An old man was making chai. He was good-looking and amiable. After handing me a hot cup, he sat down on the chair next to mine. I was curious so I asked him a few frivolous questions. He said, 'I'm from Itawa. Nobody asks me anything, and I never listen to anyone. I belong to a lower caste, so going to school was out of the question.'

We were silent for some time. He was gazing in the distance, perhaps where the sky met the valley. He was smoking a *bidi* and, after a long pause, spoke in English, 'I just wanted to live a little more than everyone.'

I was shocked. Then I looked at the chair he was sitting on.

'You should sit here; that chair is broken.'

He looked at me and smiled again, 'I've always got broken chairs in my life. They don't let you sit for long.' He chuckled. 'I always feared a good chair, you know. It would make me comfortable, and it would be hard to let it go. And if someone does take it, I'll have to keep standing for the rest of my life.' There was a gay abandon in his voice. The chai he made was passable, and there was nothing to eat in the shop.

'By the way, the chair you're sitting on is broken too.' We both burst out laughing. And our laughter rang through the mountains and boomeranged back to us.

I used to tell myself, 'I am happy', as an excuse. Even when I was not, I kept repeating the words until the feeling started to seep in. I was biking in the mountains and crossing remote villages. Every new place made me happier than the previous one.

Nights were spent in unknown places, but the stars changed everything. The sky looked different every night. I would blink my eyes to make sure that I wasn't dreaming. The stars seemed so close that if I jumped high enough, I could snatch one if I tried. One can't be sure where the stars in the sky end and where the village lights begin.

And then the next day, the magic began again. Ah, the Himalayas! I look at the majestic mountains and think about something I had to say but forgot. Oh! I forgot to repeat that I am happy. But the false happiness had dropped away long ago. I cleaned my bike for the next ride when an old man opened his chai shop. It was called *hansmukh* (happy-go-lucky) chai shop. I asked for a hansmukh chai so I could start my journey again.

I heard the silence as I lazed in the forests of Kumaon. It takes time to develop an ear to listen to it. The beautiful town of Almora was in front of me, with the Panchachuli mountain range dominating the background. Mukteshwar was now behind me.

I recalled that Nirmal Verma had talked about this trail in one of his writeups. He used to walk from Mukteshwar to Almora on this old path. In his book, *Maneaters of Mukteshwar*, Jim Corbett mentioned this trail as well. Just now, in this silence, I saw Nirmal and Corbett walking together. Amazing. I think I need food. My hunger is making me delusional. Am I here or not?

Today, I reached Koofadaa, Hansa's (Sooraj, who played 'Hansa' in the movie *Hansa*) home. Deepal (his father) and I sat in the sun and talked about unimportant things. As the sun shifted, casting a shadow on us, a shiver ran through my body. My eyes looked for a spot in the sun while Deepal's eyes were set on a room behind us.

'That was Hansa's room,' he said after a long pause. I knew that his heart was about to burst with sadness. He was searching for a crack, an opening, to let it all out. With these words, he'd found it.

'It happened last year,' he started, remembering the date, weather, and time of the day as if it was a few hours ago. If he stopped or got absorbed in his thoughts, a voice from behind would nudge him to go on. It was Hansa's mother, living the same story with her husband.

'This is the place where he drank the poison.' Deepal stood up after saying this, 'I picked him up, put him on my shoulders and ran downhill.' The road was two kilometres away from the house. His voice grew sombre with the pain of a father who couldn't save his young son. His son, Hansa, had received the best actor award in New York for the film.

Deepal's eyes were sunken and dry, making him look way older than his years. He visits government offices with a petition to build a road through his village. 'Had there been a road, I would have got another ten minutes.' I wanted to tell him that if there is a road, the forest will become a resort. But a father would not have been able to listen to this.

The day was getting colder, but I had stopped shivering. The three of us were silent now. The forest around us was quiet. The birds, balled up and still, were hanging from a tree; still like the mourning mountains that stood with bent shoulders—tired mountains—loaded with Hansa's voice. This stillness, this quietude in the mountains makes your belly hurt.

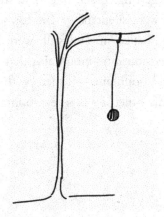

As the mountains envelop me with their majesty
My head bows down in shame.
While these giants touch me with beauty
I am still stuck with my name.
For thousands of years, its oaks and pines
Have welcomed men like me.
They chuckle at the words I say
And so will the wind that flows between.
Will these mountains still be there
When I have gone away?
Their secret songs will still play on
And I fear I will miss it all, again.

I knew London through its theatres. Whenever I stepped out of the cinema, my head buzzed with beautiful pictures, actors, stories and colours. Then, with the London Theatre guide in my hand, I would plan my next adventure. I ate a little and lay down in the park often. Then, after my short nap, I would head to Curzon Theatre for the next show. Oh, how I loved it! I didn't realize how still I became. I hadn't spoken a single word for a very long time. So quiet was I that even the faintest of images left a strong impression on me. And as I carried that effect in my heart into the Tube, I couldn't help but look at the people around me differently. I was present with it all in more senses than one and yet not fully there.

I cannot say goodbye.

I don't know how to do it. How can you say it ends 'here'? Because the 'here' you see is just the tip of the iceberg, while 'there' is where the rest of it lies. So, when it stops 'here', what happens to all that was 'there' inside of me? I guess I'm just a coward, and being a writer has helped me be one.

Meanwhile, Scotland is beautiful.

As I watch my sorrows drown in a beautiful lake one by one, a wish appears—to have come here sooner. There is so much beauty to be seen in the world that I fear I started late. And so afraid am I to miss out that I try to eat more than I can digest like a hungry child. But I guess I am hungry for everything.

I am happy.

And as soon as I say it, I've left happiness behind. A dash towards something else—darkness? I want to get back to that feeling, so I ask my driver, Zafar, 'Do you think I'm happy?'

He looks at me before replying, 'You do look happy in your pictures.'

That's right. I start looking at other people's pictures. Everybody looks happy in photographs.

'Let's go to the place where this city began, Zafar,' I request, hoping to find a spot where everything was happy—like the first day of a relationship.

Zafar drives me to Loch Lomond, and I look at the city from there. How strange. It's my last day in the city, and I am standing at its beginning. I thought this would ease my burdens. Little did I realize that journeys, while taking our sorrows away, add something back too.

And so, I wouldn't be surprised if one day, long after I am gone, my sorrows become moss and start floating on the surface of that beautiful lake.

Even though New York had begun to feel like my own, riding the metro was a different story. I long to talk to people, and all of them seemed busy right now. Perhaps that was the reason I still felt disconnected on the train. So, I closed my eyes. When I opened them again, the coach was almost empty. I looked at my watch—I'd been asleep for about twenty minutes! An old Englishman was sitting next to me, scribbling something in a small notebook. I had missed my station. I was lost again. Sensing my nervousness, the old man turned to me and explained how to get back. In the end, he added, 'And finally, you will take the path you were supposed to take.'

'Are you a writer?' I asked. He laughed and then replied, 'A famous one.'

I felt excited, 'I'm a writer too. Although not a famous one.'

His laugh turned to a smile now, 'So, how's life?'

I replied without skipping a beat, 'Life is good. In fact, very good.'

He was happy to hear my answer and then enquired if I had written about that.

'Written about what?'

'That life is good,' his face sombre now.

I was silent for a while before I replied, 'No.'

He closed his little notebook and looked at me directly, 'Whenever I go back to my old diaries, all I see is sadness, depression and complaints. I remember in moments of despair; I pressed ink on paper. But now, when I read them, it feels like I've had a very sad life. And that isn't true. I forgot to note down moments when I had said that life is good. And that is my advice to you. Don't forget to register the times when you say, "Life is good".'

I was speechless. And then he added, 'You may get off on this station.'

The spell, now broken, released me. I got off. On the platform, I realized I had forgotten to ask his name. So, I looked back and shouted, 'What's your name?' He looked at me, but the train had already started moving. I could see that he was smiling. We both looked at each other and shrugged.

I always long to read a new writer—to read words that ring so true that it's hard to decipher if they were written for the world or only for me. I yearn to feel so close that it feels like the writer has taken a seat next to mine and has started whispering into my ears. So palpable is the feeling that I am being led into a deep river to get soaked in the warm water where every word is alive and can do anything—even birth songs out of disasters. The world becomes a wet painting with a thick coat of colours, and it's not just the canvas that changes.

When I find such a book, the rest of my days with it are filled with ecstasy. But, when I don't, I am hounded by the feeling of separation from words that could have resonated with my heart. Maybe this search leads one to write what they have been looking for. This longing rips the heart open, and out pours a poem, a story or a play. And it's only later that one realizes that everything has changed.

I still have faith that if you hold marble against the sun, you can see the whole universe inside it. And on the other hand, I believe that a firefly lives not when it glows but, in the darkness, in between two twinkles. And whenever my life's sun starts burning my shoulders and the burden seems too heavy to bear, the thoughts of the fireflies and the marble provide some shade of relief. I sense a cool breeze touching my face, and I start writing about *Tathagat* (the second film I made) sitting in the mountains and I start feeling cold.

A small bird plays on the gooseberry tree these days. The trees have covered the sky, and I can't see the eagles any more. It is better this way. Because when I see the eagles, I end up thinking about my old houses. And try as I may, I can't shake the memories away. So, I don't look for eagles any more.

If you pretend to laugh, you eventually end up laughing; the same way, if you pretend well, it can pull happiness basking on the gooseberry tree. But then, a pair of squirrels start running on the tree's trunk, tiny red ants start marching in a straight line, and I start thinking about my unfinished stories. It's hard to add even a single word to them. Perhaps some of these stories will remain unfinished. I will always regret the time I decided to get up from my desk while writing. One wishes to have never left, to have finished all unfinished business. But new stories don't start where old ones end. They somehow know the pain of incompleteness and die before their time. That is why I have stopped struggling to write.

Now, I wait for that little bird that plays on the gooseberry tree. It comes and goes. While waiting for it, I see a squirrel running in the same spot. I notice that the ants don't walk in a line anymore. The moment I stop looking for the bird, it appears. I see happiness sitting on the gooseberry tree . . .

how small it is and how much it gives me. I forget everything when I look at it. I forget that behind this dense tree is a blue sky where eagles still fly. And an unfinished story would be waiting on my desk. So, I set everything aside and pick a gooseberry. And it is then that I realize that happiness is not seeing the bird but in the hope of it. In all my unfinished stories is the hope of a new one. And I can be free from the struggle of finding it because I know it will appear when I stop looking.

Let's think of a different story today. A different story starts with a vision of the river. Let's start from there—a river. A holy man is sitting under a peepul tree on the riverbank. He's reading the lines on a young boy's palm.

'There is danger lurking by,' he warns and stares at the sky, 'Only God can help.'

Suddenly, a girl jumps down from the tree—adjusting her dupatta. She looks young, probably on the threshold of puberty. The holy man sees that the boy is holding on to the other end of the girl's dupatta. The parrot in the cage shrieks, 'Same old story . . . same old story', and a voice vibrates from the tree, 'Why don't you change it?'

This voice makes the holy man angry. So, he snatches the dupatta out of the boy's hand and ties him to the tree with it. Soon, the holy man begins running behind the girl. This makes the parrot happy, and the leaves start falling from the tree.

In time we would know that the holy man fell so in love with the girl that he shaved off his beard and became a young boy. And the boy tied to the tree grew a beard. He started taking care of the parrot in the cage. The tree grew. And from then on, whenever the parrot tried saying, 'same old story', a whistle came out instead.

I am getting old . . . There is a mango tree in the distant future. This older man sees the mango tree. Now, he's sitting on the tree, eating mangoes. I wake up.

The dream manages to make me smile in my otherwise monotonous life. The simplicity of it all is enchanting. The bookshelf stuffed with stories waits for me to take one out. I pick a book and start reading. It seems like I started the story in my dream already. It feels close, so close like I touched it last night. I make chai, unaware if I'm living my dream or reality. I sit on the balcony as if I am sitting on the tree. There is chai in my hand instead of the mango and the dream-like book is being read by an old man.

'I am not the one you see; I am the one who writes.' The thought entered my mind, and I felt like writing it down. I opened my phone and started typing. There's a joy in writing anything anywhere. The moment it finishes, I will post it on Instagram. It feels like I've launched a rocket in space—a message sent to the universe. Who will read it and where? I do not know. But the freedom of writing that I feel is freeing. It's like a journey. Everything can feel just as it is. It is like taking out layer after layer as if peeling an onion—I know I will find nothing in the end, and yet here I am.

Nirmal and Vinod—how simple and beautiful these two names are, both my favourite writers. Although I could never meet Nirmal Verma, I had the fortune of meeting Vinod Kumar Shukla. I remember looking for his home in Raipur. As soon as I found his name, it took my breath away. All his stories came rushing in. I was star-struck. I rang the bell and entered a different world. The friend who was accompanying me faded away. After a while, Vinod Kumar Shukla appeared. He was standing in front of me in a torn vest and trunks. I wondered if it was him or a character from his stories. I looked at his feet and instinctively bowed down to touch them. He was embarrassed. 'Come in and have a seat, you two; I'll get dressed,' he said and left. We entered and sat down. It was a simple room with no decorations except a painting of the poet Muktibodh. I remembered when I had called Vinod ji and begun shaking when I heard him at the other end. I had spoken some gibberish in English and was getting restless with myself; I had put the phone down with 'I love you.' I was feeling embarrassed while thinking about it when he appeared again. He had put on a pair of simple pants.

'How are you?' I began the conversation.

'I am good. It's just that I don't keep so well these days,' he replied. I started worrying about his health. I was still looking at the holes in his vest.

After a pause, he looked at me and said, '*Dekho Manav yatharth to jhooth hai, Kalpana sach hai* [Manav, what we see is deception, imagination is the truth].' Hearing those words, I fell apart from the inside. I couldn't hear anything after that. His wife came in with chai and biscuits after a while . . . I felt that this is not real. She was also a character from his stories that had jumped in from the window, and he was just calling her his wife.

He sincerely listened to me reciting his poem, *Hatasha Se Ek Vyakti* (Youtube: Hindi Kavita), and said afterwards, 'I was not listening to my poem; I was listening to you.' His eyes had become moist. I couldn't tell him how much I loved him. I think he doesn't even realize how ardently people admire his writing. When I handed him my first book, *Theek Tumhare Peeche* (Right Behind You), I realized my hands were shaking. He read the preface and said, 'It is good.'

'No, Vinod ji, this is all farce . . .only you are the truth,' I said sheepishly.

He is like a roaring river, and I am just a bowl of dirty water. Meeting him felt like finding shade in the scorching heat. After we bid him farewell, my friend said, 'Did you realize that you were shaking all this while? You couldn't even say one proper sentence.' Honestly, I hadn't remembered anything. I asked, 'Did I tell him that I loved him?' and I was relieved when he said, 'Yes, many times.'

My father sat with my book *Theek Tumhare Peeche* in his hands. He was trying to read every word through a lens. His eyesight had weakened over the years. So much so that he had to use a lens along with his glasses. I went over to him and thought about stopping him. You won't understand these stories, I wanted to say. But he was so engrossed that I didn't distract him. So, I made up my mind to leave. I was about to step out when he noticed me. I don't think he recognized my face. His questioning eyes sent chills down my bones. He started reading again. I hurried outside.

My father is a man of simple thinking. He never understood acting, writing or playwriting. We hardly talked about any of it. I don't think he ever came to see my plays either. I liked that about him. He never did anything which he wasn't inclined to. But then why did he have my book in his hands now? It made me question his existence in my work. I've built him and destroyed him repeatedly. In the end, I've found him in those works as well. I understand that it is all fiction. But does he? My father is a simple man, He doesn't understand fiction.

Worried, I ran to the room and said, '*Pitaji*, this is all fiction. It is not real. It didn't happen. Do you understand that?' His eyes left the page and rested on me. 'Do you think what you're living is real?' I kept looking at him and realized, I was seeing him for the first time.

Strangely, the person who loses wins our hearts in most stories. It's as if we share a common history of loss. We show off our victories while making life-long secrets of our defeats. But our wins, after a while, seem hollow. And when the false covers slip, it is defeat that stares right into our eyes. So, we get up and leave the *mehfil*.

On the other hand, people find our lives beautiful, as if looking at a house from the outside. Little do they know that these beautiful houses have store rooms where our downfalls remain hidden. When we decide that a thing is worth hiding, it also becomes intensely intimate. We all have had our share of losses. We all have such beautiful houses that are filled with unfinished business. Maybe that is the reason why the losers in stories become so dear to us. The wins look so unfamiliar and the losses so dear!

I'm stepping out in the rain to look for a good book. When I stay at home for too long and then decide to step out wearing my *chappals*, I see the shoes lying in there as well. I haven't worn them in a long time. I think about the long journeys when I look at them and remember my feet haven't been inside them for a while. It makes me uncomfortable. I am not old enough—to walk in them or to write a novel. Chappals are free—like short stories, they let me wander. I can venture out and still make it back home in time. But it is the poems and plays which are like walking barefoot. I don't even have to step out to create something. They are comfortable in the boundaries of a home and so am I. For now. I feel this is not my age to write novels, but I'm addicted to long journeys. If you can't write, you can read one at least. So, I placated the shoes and told the chappals to tell the shoes we were going to buy a novel. If we find a good writer in the rain, then it's sure to be a long journey.

As the story ends, I feel like I have betrayed someone. It is as if I've let out a secret that had been living between us for a long time. I used this friendship to my advantage, and now its sanctity is lost. But more significant still is the betrayal of the story. It was as if we were living inside each other, but by writing the end, I have killed it. This is the kind of violence that makes me feel guilty. But when the guilt leaves, the sadness of everyday life takes over. And I must enter the ordinary world again.

Some plays never find a meaningful ending, some poems are sacrificed to logical reasoning and some stories hurt at the slightest touch. And then I think about the times I've spent with blank pages. Sometimes, I've lived a whole story, yet not a single word made it to the paper. Such stories put a smile on my face. They are the purest ones, untouched by the outside world.

Today, as I sit in the Indian Coffee House in Kolkata, an old story shows up. I wondered if she remembered I was writing a story for her in this place. She was sitting across from me, and I was hoping to read it to her once I was done. It had to be a different story. But I could never finish it. In my story, I wrote, 'and she returns'. In real life, she did not. And so, I didn't find meaning in continuing the story.

Years later, here I am, sitting in the same coffee shop, in the same spot. I'm staring at the empty chair in front of me. A thought crosses my mind; maybe I should scratch off 'she returns' and replace it with 'and she leaves'. This way, the story will come to an end and leave me for good. But what if I leave it as is, unfinished and keep it sacred? Forever.

The evening was without joy. I left my house, and the city seemed to invite me with its bright lights. The sky was changing colours—red, orange and purple. The last few days had been challenging, and I felt heavy because of their after-effects. I tell myself, 'Life is very simple' in times like these. I walk with this consolation as much as I can, and when I can't take it anymore, I return home. Lying in my bed, I stared at the ceiling and divided my worries in two. The dreams that had a minuscule chance of coming true went to the left of the ceiling fan. Those that were rebellious and I could not control, went to the right. When I looked, they seemed content with the little pleasures of life like the chirping of birds, sipping chai in bed, resolving not to smoke and still lighting a cigarette or a cat entering the room.

It is late now; my last cup of chai has pulled me out of sleep. So, I flip pages of Arundhati's books and find myself in Old Delhi.

I have been reading the letters between Paul Auster and J.M. Coetzee for some time. The book is called *Here and Now*. I love the title. How did these two great authors write about simple things like games, writing, economics, friendship and getting old? I read the book as if I have received a letter just now. I read Paul's reply/letter in the morning and Coetzee's with my evening chai. Why do I read Coetzee in the evening? I don't know. I never read Paul's letters in the evenings. Some writers are like the music we like to wake up to. One does not want to mix this music with the end of the day. I have become like a postman; not a postman, but a letterbox.

It is 3 a.m., and it has started to rain.

I smiled after writing the 'letterbox'. I ran to the balcony and then remembered that I had left my cup of chai on the table. I returned with the cup and sat on the balcony. A spray of rainwater touched my face. There was complete silence in the colony. I started paying attention to the little noises I could hear. The gooseberry tree was shedding its leaves; below the balcony was a carpet of yellow. I came back inside as if I had remembered something and started reading Van Gogh's letters. The book is called *Have Faith in Me: The Letters of Vincent Van Gogh (Mujh pe Bharosa Rakhna)*. I have developed a strange habit of gathering myself now. It's like I need to sweep and pick up every part of me that was scattered.

I woke up at 2.35 a.m. If I had decided to go back to sleep, I would have gathered my scattered pieces, but I woke up. I started writing, made chai and started listening to this silence. At some point, I will go down and look at the sunrise. There is a chai shop at the gate that opens at five in the morning. Whenever he sees me walking towards him, he smiles. Initially, I thought that he was laughing at me (being alone in this city can be embarrassing at times). But I was wrong. He is a person who gets excited quickly. Whenever he sees someone like me in the morning, he gets excited. The rain has stopped now, and voices of coughing and gargling from other houses take over. This city is beginning to wake up. I decided that this morning I will ask the chaiwallah his name. Only his name . . . And I will read him Paul's letter as if it was written for me.

Suddenly it feels like I've slept through many days. I feel strange when I look at the date. These last few days were lost in a haze. I can recollect some things, but others are lost as if submitted to the darkness. Does this mean I've lost them forever? Does it mean that I will never see them in this lifetime again? My heart decides to skip a beat; my hands rise to caress my forehead. My body takes a deep breath in, and the corners of my eyes start to water. This happens when your name catches me unaware. 'O my Kavita [poem] . . .', the end of a serious love affair and poetry are similar for me; I have stuffed them in between plays, stories and acting. I cannot write it again. It's as if the shoes I bought with you have started biting me. No, they were uncomfortable before, too, but at least we were together. And they reminded me of you. But now you are gone. And these shoes don't fit anyway. Just like my old home cannot live in my new house anymore. I have an urge to pick up some pages and try. I want to bind you down and write you into a poem once again. I can feel you. I can smell you. I know you are waiting for me to touch the pages. But I cannot write poems anymore. Do you even know how cruel it was to leave without notice? I kept on staring at the blank pages for days; I kept looking for you in the evenings and waiting for you in the nights too. You did not return. When others started reciting poems, I became mad with envy. They had you. But weren't you only mine?

Then I realized that you never stay in one place for long. So, I devised a new way to meet you—I touch you in my stories and see you in my acting. We sit together, have chai and talk. After a while, I ask you to leave. You don't feel too bad. I don't feel too sorry.

A Very Easy Death by Simone de Beauvoir.

'Whether you think of it as heavenly or as earthly, if you love life, immortality is no consolation for death.'

The day slips in and out between my mother's dreams. It drags from the familiarity of her face to the strangeness of not recognizing her. Death walks around the one who gave you life, yet you cannot do anything to stop it. However, you can pray for an easy death, pray that she goes silently and peacefully. And even this prayer comes with a pang of guilt.

It is natural for an old person to die, but how Simone describes the last days of her mother's life makes it palpable for us. 'When someone you love dies, you pay for the sin of outliving her with a thousand piercing regrets.' In the final pages, the sisters are dividing their mother's things after she's passed away. Simone's sister wants to keep the ribbons. How do you fill the space left by the person who died? We always feel that we have the skill to do something about it. But every failed attempt makes us realize the futility of listening to our voice in that space. A parent's death is something that we have all imagined at least once, and yet we can never be prepared for. Whenever Simone writes about Room Number 114 in the book, I feel as if I am standing in front of that room.

I remember I went to see Pandit Satyadev Dubey in the hospital. He was in a coma. This was a few days before his death. I stood there for a long time and suddenly felt the urge to put my hand on his forehead. When he was alive, I could never imagine doing such a thing. I thought he had had a bad dream. The moment I touched his forehead, I started crying uncontrollably and couldn't stop for a long time.

When I was reading *A Very Easy Death*, I remembered touching Dubey ji's forehead. I don't know why I was embarrassed about crying then! 'There is no such thing as a natural death. Nothing that ever happens to a man is natural, since his presence calls the whole world into question. All men must die, but for every man his death is an accident, and even if he knows it he would sense it as an unjustifiable violation.'

Morning.

I like waking up early in the morning. While my room rests in darkness, I watch specks of light enter it softly. A sparrow starts chirping on my windowsill. I feel happy. I can hold this feeling all day in my heart. These are the small things—like watching a dewdrop balance on a leaf, a squirrel during the most critical leaps, catching the cat in the middle of mischief—all of these are wonders that leave a smile on my face and I can hold on to it for long.

Because I've always stayed in small rooms, I find myself drawn to smaller things. I never liked sunrises or sunsets. These are big for me. I like watching the light play with smaller things.

I remembered a morning unfolding in Nainital years ago. An old man swept the roads as the shutters of the tiny shops rolled up. The air was filled with morning prayers from a temple far away. I still remember those prayers. This morning was like a morning in Pune and yet felt so different. Newspaper boys zoomed on their bicycles, milkmen shuffled their milk cans, making a clinking sound and the first bird lazily chirped before dawn—everything seemed like the making of a play. These were the morning characters. They can be anywhere in the world, be it a village, a town or a big city. It's the same morning scene, although the characters are different and start their day in various ways. However, the beginning seems familiar. It excites me. I get giddy when a play begins; it doesn't matter if I'm writing it or watching it. It's permanently impregnated with a sense—of possibilities.

Afternoon.

I like afternoons as well. They fondly remind me of my village. Six families lived in a big compound. Afternoons were like festivals. Games being played in the shade, secrets pushed in the darkest corners, hide and seek, doctor-doctor, office-office, talking to a cat for a long time and a river. No, not the entire river but just a small piece of its shores.

I remember the afternoon when I wrote the first lines of *Shakkar ke Paanch Daane* (Five Grains of Sugar), '*Main lad Raha hu* [I am fighting].' Almost all my plays have started in the languor of afternoons, and somehow, I remember the exact time I started writing them. I even remember the music that was playing in the background. It is strange that although I enjoy watching a morning unfold, all my works begin in the afternoons. I saw ants marching in a straight line on my balcony yesterday. I got excited! I wanted to see their beginning and end until an ant caught my eye. It seemed to deviate from the rules of being an ordinary ant. Its gait was slower, and it didn't care about following the line.

Trying to be an average human seems like following the line too. How scary is it to slow down, deviate and not do what everybody is doing?

Evening.

Most of my evenings are spent walking. I have realized that I form my relationships in the evening, as with Krishna, the pastry guy in McLeod Ganj. I used to spend almost all my evenings with him. He was so innocent that we would end up laughing at his innocent talks. Like the way he demanded that Hanuman drop his *gada* (mace) and do something for him every evening!

I met Hansa in the mountains of Uttarakhand. The forests became more interesting to him.

And then there is this man who sells gol gappas on the street close to my house. He seems like a character from one of Beckett's absurd plays. There is no logic in our conversations.

When I say, 'I was feeling lonely since the morning,' he replies, 'Yeah, I'm sorry the water was too spicy today.'

If I say, 'Have you seen this film?' he says, 'It rained, and I couldn't set up my stall. Were you looking for me?'

I like spending time with him. I can disclose my best-kept secrets, and his replies somehow make perfect sense. After spending the whole day, people want to talk to someone about it, especially before the night. Maybe that is the reason why I've found the most beautiful friends in the evenings.

Night.

The night is like slowed down music. I do not switch on the lights until every ounce of the day has left the room. It feels like the ending of a play—fade out. Add some good music, and you have a good end.

I get up and make coffee, not chai. I have spent most of my nights reading books and sipping coffee. What's a better time to finish a long-overdue story than this? Sometimes, I re-read stories. I have seen them becoming mine when I touch them the second time. Life starts oozing out from the pages. But I do not stay up late. The excitement of the following morning makes me want to sleep early. After a slow-burning cigarette, a drink, a book and some music, I am fast asleep.

Morning again.

I woke up early today. The sunlight has started to enter my room, and so has the chirping of birds and mutterings of pigeons. Two eagles are gliding in the sky. Seven birds sit on the tree outside. I started reading *Notes from a Small Room* again and this is how they go—

'Happiness is as exclusive as a butterfly, and you must never pursue it. If you stay very still, it may come and settle on your hand. But only briefly. Savour those moments, for they will not come in your way very often.'—Ruskin Bond.

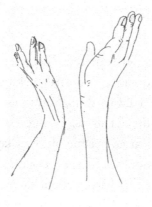

Why is everything so scattered? 'Let's set everything right first'—with this thought, I started making my house look more like a home. I always thought that all it takes is to clean it and peel off all the old layers. Then, everything would look new. But when I started peeling off these layers, I uncovered some cracks. How do you fill these cracks? I planned to write about them. Maybe, if I write about them well, I can fill all these spaces. And once they are filled, my house will be as good as the home of my childhood. So, I started writing, but wait! Now some dark corners that I didn't know existed appeared. Many strange stories were hiding in those corners. My writing had stirred things up and had cracked the walls even more. The house was taking a toll on my writing. It was in shambles, and sunrays could pass through the walls. Nothing can stay for long in this house. That's the tragedy of being a writer. You use up all the things in your writing that could've helped you build a home.

The smell of a new book! It's morning. I don't start reading a book immediately, I smell it for some time. In a while I hear the clearing of a throat and I see the writer take a seat. I don't read, I wait—for his first peg to finish, his first long smoke . . . and for him to turn towards me. I wait. I wait until I can feel the writer come close to me and decide to start whispering the story in my ear. By now I've finished reading the preface and it's time to start the journey with this human who has written this book. I start reading the book.

'This is free; you can take it home if you want,' the waiter mumbled as he put a few packets of Sugar Free on my table.

'I don't want it,' I replied curtly, showing my distaste for anything free.

'What if you change your mind?' He was unfazed.

I suddenly felt exposed. He knew me better. I looked at the packets and wondered if I did need some Sugar Free. Perhaps I could use it. I may put it in my morning chai or my evening coffee and maybe even improve my health. Suddenly, a free thing gathered worth and claimed a place in my world. Had he kept a stone there, I would have started needing it too. Could I claim this morning and place it in my living room if that is the case? Or could I borrow the face of that anxious man sitting across the café? I wanted to talk to him, but that could increase his anxiety. Had he decided to make the first move, for example, smile at me or just nod, I would've done the rest. But he ignored me. I didn't exist for him. He didn't even look at me when I walked in. I let go of my need for his attention and shifted my gaze outside. A bus full of people waited at the roadside. It looked like a café by itself—many people sitting side by side with nothing in common but an agreement to ignore each other.

Why are we like this? I looked at myself. Why am I like this? Why am I so distant from everyone? Do people stop existing if you don't know them? I started feeling anxious. Or it might have been the coffee. It tasted good in the morning, but I felt restless as I gulped down the third cup. I began to scribble, but everything that came out was either childish or boorish. Finally, I realized that I am writing what I'm not, like faking sickness with a healthy body. I left the free Sugar Free on the table and imagined the space it might have taken in my world. If I could fill that space with anything, shouldn't it be with a morning? This gave the needy writer in me food for thought and I stepped out from the coffee house.

Before every battle, I wonder what is at stake here.

Our battles are also very strange! Like should I have coffee in the morning or the same old chai? Should I wear shoes this time instead of chappals? Should I walk fast or slow, should I get out of bed or lie around some more? These small decisions, just like the big decisions in our lives, are hanging on for a moment. Both have one thing in common—what's at stake? The question echoes in one's head. But the question is not the problem. The problem begins when you answer it. The moment you choose one option, the other starts troubling the mind. The chosen one comes and becomes a part of our tired lives.

Just like right now. I have chai, but I'm thinking about coffee. I have brought a book called *The Naïve and Sentimental Novelist* from inside while *Kafka on the Shore* is on the bed. I have Orhan Pamuk in my hand as Murakami haunts my mind . . . isn't it a conflicting situation? I stopped sipping chai. I went inside. Made coffee. Came out with coffee and Murakami.

But you can't do such a thing with big decisions. Now, Pamuk and Murakami, as well as chai and coffee, are before me. With all these options in front of me, I am more confused than ever. I'm enjoying neither chai nor coffee. Reading neither Pamuk nor Murakami. And I start laughing. Not having much can keep life beautifully simple.

In this stillness, an altogether different thought started swimming in my head.

When you are in a crowded place, you always long for space. But when you have it, what do you do? Isn't it hypocrisy? Whenever I start thinking about journeys and locking my house, I dream about returning and opening my door again. Opening the door is the other point. This creates time and space. Locking my house is the first. My journey between these two points is nothing but fiction. Everything turns into a story whose beginning is closing the door, and the end opens it again. Then who is the one who goes on the journey? It is not I. I am the one closing and opening the door. Should I lock the door? What's at stake?

I spent the whole afternoon staring at my screen. I wanted today to be the day—the day when I accomplished something. Instead, my fingers touched the delete button, and everything I had ever written returned to the same nothingness it had come from. Nothing was left but a blank page. Still, I have no idea why, it felt as if some work had been done. I felt satisfied. I walked out of the discomfort that I had been feeling for the past week. I also walked out of remorse—no reason to be sad anymore! A man burdened with his own decisions stood beside me. We decided to pull out everything from the darkness, gamble with the universe and maybe remake history. My fingers started thumping the keyboard. The black dots began making love to the white pages, and the man whispered, 'Here you go again, phantom! The world is yours.'

Virginia Woolf's writing leaves an impression on one's mind. The words echo long after one has finished. When read constantly, her work makes one see things very closely. Like patterns—something that I've been thinking about a lot since this morning. When we write, this is what we notice the most. The overpowering emotion can tie us down with an illusion. The only way to save ourselves is to write about it and struggle our way out from it. All our writings in that time are strangely tied to what we felt in that period. As we continue writing, patterns start appearing. It may feel like going in circles for some time until a thread starts connecting everything. Maybe that's what Virginia Woolf talks about.

We end up writing about the things that bother us the most. But the lives we are living are exactly the ones we had imagined once upon a time. Even if we try hard and live differently, we create patterns that fit into where we want to be.

There is another thing that I was reading in the morning that resembled the same idea. In Manglesh Dabral's *Lekhak ki Roti* (The Writer's Bread), it is written, 'How I wish us poets were smugglers or thieves. Then one day we would have witnessed the killing/death of a crane like Valmiki, and like him, a poem would have spontaneously poured out of our mouths, making us great poets. Or I wish we were a prince who decided to leave everything and find enlightenment upon seeing the sadness and death in the world. But nothing magical happened. We couldn't ascend our normal, daily human life.' (I have selected only a few lines). The other thing that I find highly intriguing is that all our hurt, pain, stubbornness, miracles, happiness, all these are so . . . mundane. That is an apt word. It could have been momentary, but the term has various other meanings. When an emotion affects us for a long time, it becomes part of our writing, and the pattern settles into our everyday lives.

We go about our days walking side by side with grief. It is tempting to let that grief become anger aimed at someone else. How easily that anger can come back to us.

What is that force that makes us work at this moment? I want to hold its pattern. Look! I can't even stop thinking about it. I don't want to return to where I created my last work. I believe that whatever we make reflects all the patterns of our lives at that time. Our likes, dislikes, our character . . . everything is visible. If I want to change the way I write or direct, I will have to change myself. But how much do I know about change? And suddenly, it dawns upon me that I'm feeling all of this because I had read Virginia Woolf before I fell asleep last night. How powerful is her writing! Will I ever be able to come close to that?

While sitting with a few Korean artists yesterday, I began the conversation with a question, 'Why do we create? Or why do we write?' The question came up probably because I was struggling with the thought for some time. I had a few superficial and oft-repeated answers to it. We sat in silence for some time. There were four of us—Janghai (songwriter), Sook (painter), Haiyon (writer) and I. The silence prevailed for two reasons. One, that which was obvious and second because none of them spoke English fluently. Finally, Haiyon responded. She said she thinks that we all have an island inside of us, a beautiful secret place. When we talk about that place, inevitably, stories appear. And because she didn't want to talk to anyone about those stories, she liked to write them.

Then we jumped to the topic of the loneliness every artist faces. In that empty space that is inside of us where whatever we keep, multiplies. Like a patch of grass, it can turn into a jungle when left unchecked. We can then harvest a story, weave a painting or create a song.

I had seen Sook's paintings. She used to paint the particles of emotions. At least, that was what I could understand from the broken conversations we'd had. Amongst all this, Janghai remained serious, although she's a very energetic woman.

Soon, they started talking amongst themselves in Korean apologizing to me every now and then. To me, their language was music. I stared at the mountains while listening to their melody.

After a while, when they had finished, they apologized again and began looking at me as if they had answered my question. I felt like they must've given an answer.

My next question was, 'What do we do about our loneliness when we have no use for it?' To make them understand, I explained that almost all young artists in Toji live with a certain degree of loneliness. They have been given such a beautiful place to create, yet no one is around when they finish the day's work and get up. In this situation, they have two choices: either make more or vanish in the jungles of solitude.

Janghai seemed a bit angry with this question. She wanted to say something, but nothing came out of her mouth. Finally, she composed herself and said, 'It's a lie to write about hunger when you've never been hungry, and it's a lie to write about loneliness when you've never been alone.' She was visibly moved as she finished her sentence. Everyone was looking at her, surprised. She seemed to have been also taken aback a bit. Then she got up and left.

After some time, all of us were alone in our respective rooms. I knew what Janghai was trying to say. I also did not have a response. When we chose to be artists, we chose this life. Then who is to be blamed? The age when we decided to be artists? Or the person who has never come in our lives but takes our pens from us and breaks them?

'You don't understand this now. But you'll regret it later,' these wise words have haunted me for years. I've waited for that 'later' so that I can finally regret it. But it's nowhere to be seen. I feel sad when I meet people in a space where loneliness seems endless. It's happened to me as well. When there was not a soul around. And I was the only one who had to deal with it.

When I asked Haiyon how she dealt with loneliness, she said that she spent that time with her favourite characters. She lives with them, talks to them and nurtures them. She enjoys walking on her secret island.

I liked her explanation. What is the cost of our loneliness? It may be the companionship of all the characters we had found while playing hide-and-seek. But the tragedy is that these characters are with us only till we write them. The moment they are on the page, they disappear from our lives. And that is the reason why some writers never finish their work.

What sort of plays are we performing? Do we even understand plays?

For instance, the dawn is a scene where it all begins. There is a fade-in every morning and our life fills with possibilities. As the day ends, we either have a fabulous scene or sometimes a single word or sometimes a full stop. But the real play is never revealed. We are so deep in it that we live as if it's real.

So, where is it? The real drama is that sand that slips through our fingers. The real drama lies in the dreams that knock on our doors when we were not home. The real drama is that emptiness, which is filled by somebody else. That somebody else is time that once lost is gone forever. Honestly, the actual drama is in silence, deep breaths and pain . . . The real drama is in going away from ourselves and forgetting who we are.

In 2005, I frequented a run-of-the-mill coffee shop in old Manali. It neither had a good view nor was it popular. It simply sat in a corner, withdrawn and hidden from sight. It was almost always empty. All of this attracted me towards it. But the most significant pull came from the river that flowed next to it. Its roaring sound overpowered everything else. It also reminded me of my writing. It's hard to know when or how it will start and end. But whenever it's flowing, the thought of it leaving haunts me. One moment I am intensely writing something, and the next moment, it's gone.

I had a lot of time in hand, a notebook and a pen. So, I faithfully registered the frustrations of my everyday life. Soon, I started seeing two older men passing by the coffee shop in the evenings. Of the two, one did all the talking while the other nodded pensively. Soon, my evening chai and their evening walk started coinciding. I started waiting to see them walk by. I felt this was a ritual that concluded my day. On some days, I would have a strong urge to walk behind them and listen to their conversations. But I never could. And then, they stopped coming. Now my writing and chai had an element missing—their walks. I found that I was unable to write. I didn't even feel like having chai. I needed to find a new place for the evening. One day, as I was winding up, I saw two names written on my papers—*Bali and Shambhu* (My third play in Hindi).

I stared at them for a very long time. When I murmured these names, they seemed to breathe with energy. I could feel a play taking birth. Because I couldn't see these two men, I started writing about not seeing them. Suddenly, I was writing furiously. I almost finished my play while living in Manali. But I couldn't find an ending. I wanted to know where these men were. I asked around in a few shops and the bazaar, but nobody had ever seen them! I know I can be crazy, but this was a new height! Did they even exist? Had I just made them up?

My stay in Manali was coming to an end, and I hadn't yet finished the play. I didn't want to leave Manali without finding the end. But I have no control over my writing. It comes and goes. On the final day, as I sat on the corner seat of the bus, my heart ached. I was looking at Manali for the last time. And then I saw someone. One of the two older men was sitting in a small tea shop. I recalled he was the one who talked a lot. I felt relief wash over me; I wasn't going crazy. 'Bali,' I shouted. But why was Bali alone? He seemed sad. I knew he looked more like Shambhu? Pensive and serious. He looked straight into my eyes. There were tears in the corners of his eyes and a faint smile on his lips. I wanted to go and see him. Sit with him. But I could not. As the bus reached the small town of Mandi, the play had found its end. I had seen it floating in Bali's eyes. As I sipped

my chai, I wanted to shout out loud, 'I've finished the play!'
But I just smiled.

After that, I went to Manali many times and sat in the
same coffee shop for hours but never saw my old friends—my
Bali and Shambhu.

A little black ant was walking towards me. It had an entire empty room to walk in, but it was here, deliberately inching closer to me. I flicked it lightly with my finger. It turned around and started marching towards me again. I blew it away, but that didn't stop it. It started walking towards me again. Then, I picked it up and threw it to the other end of the room. It took a long time to regain its balance, but it started walking towards me again as soon as it was up. It was limping. I was feeling a strange kind of pain, a kind of guilt now . . . anger. As it drew closer, I flicked it hard. It flew away and lay dead. Everything was silent in the room. Suddenly its legs moved. I guess now it could walk only on two. But it started walking towards me again. I gave in.

It wasn't a black ant; it was my darkness. My pain. This time, I let it conquer me. It climbed over my body. There was a sweetness in this dark pain who would have dreamed of claiming me like this. I picked up a blank piece of paper and started writing, *Peele Scooter Wala Aadmi* (The Man with the Yellow Scooter, my second play).

I am not the man with the yellow scooter. I lack his honesty. To be him would mean being more than who I am. There was a time when stories had started to bore me. Why don't writers say what they want instead of building a story around it?

I mean, the story seems to be a crutch, and we can do without it. What a relief to say what we want to say and take away the weight of our choices, the stagnation of our excuses and the dreaminess of choosing to live despite it all. And as soon as you touch it, it flies away like a kite in the sky.

And so it happens that when we've talked about everything, we wonder if the listener understood what we didn't say. Did this person, so close to us, see the spaces between our words? These spaces wrap our relationships. They make our shadows dense. Such a shadow created the man with the yellow scooter, and although the person keeps on changing, the shadow remains the same.

When I write a play
It takes me months, at times years
To breath the words into existence,
Soak them in meaning and life.
Then a moment later
It is given away—the actors take it,
The world sees it;
It is not mine to claim.
What a pain
What a joy!
The sound of the third bell . . .
It starts pulling in the memory
Before the first scene unfurls
I see the first word appear.
It seems like a lifetime ago.
And yet every day things die,
Every day things come to life,
The sun enters the dawn
And we forget the words we say.

We will fall, slip, make mistakes, stand up and try again. For if our work finds a place in somebody's heart, it would be a win for us. The rules binding the world of theatre are as loose as these. When we're waiting for the third bell behind the stage, we inhale deeply with the thought that this would be our best show, something that we've never done before, something that will never come again. And if we end it well, it always reflects in people's eyes. It's a different kind of sparkle in the eyes, a burst of bounding laughter and everyone becomes more beautiful. On my way home from the show, I never fail to recognize that theatre makes us better people.

We were doing the first show of *Shakkar Ke Paanch Dane* (Five Grains of Sugar, my first play) in Prithvi Theater. Kumud and I were waiting for the third bell to ring. We were scared.

Kumud—There are a lot of people here.

Manav—Yes, but why? There are way too many people.

Somebody came from behind and whispered, 'It's a houseful show.'

We both looked at him angrily. As if he'd made a mistake.

Manav—No, no, it's not houseful. But, of course, he's just making that up.

Kumud—Do I remember everything?

Manav—Yes. You remember everything. Just say it slowly. Okay?

Kumud—Yes. Where's the script?

Manav—It's here, backstage.

Kumud—Yes, let it be there . . . if something goes wrong . . .

There is a signal for the third bell, and then it rings. We shake hands; I notice Kumud's hands are sweaty. We hug.

Manav—We'll do this just once Kumud bhai. Then we'll apologize to everyone and never do it again. We both nod. Kumud left for the stage.

I don't believe in magic, so I wouldn't call it that. But this is a journey of many small steps we took fearfully. That was January 2004, and we are still doing the show. We still meet on the third bell. We hug each other tightly, smile but don't say anything. We don't need those conversations anymore.

Today, while speaking in front of a room full of people at Prithvi Theater, he paused. No, he didn't forget his speech. He was only smiling. He was looking at all the people who had come to see his play. He felt like he was back in his village and standing next to the river (Narmada). He is looking at the flowing water. He is in his trunks, and telling the river of his dreams, whims and fancies. He remembers that he said he would go to Bombay one day, start working in theatre, act and make a name for himself. So scared was he that he didn't even tell his best friends. He didn't dare to think he could write a play, let alone be admired for it.

Suddenly his smile turned to laughter, and he started speaking again.

When he bowed in front of the audience in the end, the river was with him. He was bowing down to the river who had witnessed those dreams. And all those dreams that he had talked about years ago were frolicking all around him.

You must go very deep before you reach solid ground.

Don't take life too seriously, everybody suggests . . . but have we learnt to swim in shallow waters? We had to dive deep to see what lies underneath. Maybe the earth is different there. Many dreams are hidden in our secret pockets. These dreams can only splutter and break open in the deeper ground. We cannot wait for long. We must dive deep. And who knows whether we'll make it or not—we may lose our breath, drown and never see those dreams come to life. But to be afraid to jump is the saddest thing of all. We are not here to entertain anybody. We are not here to live on the surface. We will dive deep.

She was an outstanding actress. I used to follow her around. I was mesmerized by watching how easily she transformed into her role. I would ask her the same old questions about acting. She didn't answer then. She would ask me to come over for drinks, just the two of us. In her conversations, she answered all that I had asked. I was always surprised that she remembered.

'I try to look the way I am. But how am I?'

I looked at her, confused.

'*Arey!* Tell me? How am I?'

'You're excellent,' I answered hesitantly.

'To find out how I am is the reason why I act. Do you know, an entire universe lives inside of us? Yet, there is so much we still don't know about ourselves.'

'I don't feel there is anything inside me. Whatever I do, it comes out exactly the way it is.' She laughed as I complained.

'It means you haven't tasted it yet. When you do, you will look only for the good things. Every role changes the flavour. It would help if you tried it sometime. Think about what your character likes and dislikes. What does he eat? I begin working for my roles in the kitchen.'

'To do that, I would have to learn how to cook first,' I said sheepishly, and she started laughing again. How beautiful she looked!

Nowadays, I cook my food. It's been years since I've seen her. I still think that she's an exceptional actress. I get goosebumps just thinking about her. I've heard that she doesn't have much work anymore. She does a few television shows. They say that she's always irritated. We let so many actresses go because all we have for them are the trivial roles of a wife, daughter or mother. But in truth, that is our society's true reflection. Women stand on the periphery; they dare not take centre stage. What a tragedy it is—to be unable to live to your fullest! When I think of her, my heart fills with rage. When will things change?

I have an old habit of talking to Nirmal Verma. I have written down such conversations many times. The more I read and understood him, the more he became a part of me. When I write about conversations between us, things begin to resolve. Like today, when I felt uneasy. There's a play that's been in my head, but I can't seem to write it down. Suddenly, I saw Nirmal Verma sitting on the balcony, smoking a cigarette.

Manav—Nirmal, it's so late in the night . . . why are you sitting there in silence?

Nirmal—What time is it?

Manav—Almost 1 a.m. I'm trying to sleep but I'm tossing and turning.

Nirmal—These nights, impregnated with silence—they neither let the sleep come in nor the uneasiness go away.

Manav—Everything seems clogged. All the paths are closed. Every door has turned into a wall.

Nirmal—It is what it is. The more alone and unoccupied we become, the clearer things get. We can look at things minutely. We can take very small things and play with them. To stay quiet and to listen—what do you hear now?

Manav—*Haath ka aaya . . . shoonya* (the emptiness in my hand). These words have been echoing in my head for days.

Nirmal—*Shoonya*? That sounds nice.

Manav—I feel there's a whole play in this sentence.

Nirmal—But you liked writing stories. Didn't you?

Manav—I was talking about the dramatics of it.

Nirmal—Yes, as if the words say one thing and the situation another. While what we see is one thing, the sentence describes another. The conversations are happening here while the drama is somewhere else.

Manav—Exactly! This would be a new experiment. I want to do this. But how?

Nirmal—We must stop writing about things that move us—like the moon floating in the clouds, the wind blowing at night, the trees swaying in darkness, the moonlight on mountaintops and about the mountains. One should have an impression of all of this inside. It is a kind of universe that keeps things pure and alive and then turns them into words.

Manav—Your words always work. I am nursing this 'impression' inside. Whatever I will write now will speak of this.

Nirmal—What are you reading these days?

Manav—Bill Bryson and Tennessee Williams.

Nirmal—Non-fiction

Manav—I'm getting bored of fiction slowly. Stories have started to tire me. I can't read old novels anymore. Poetry seems to be lying. At least I can grasp something in non-fiction.

Nirmal—Well, fiction or non-fiction, it is the same thing after all.

Manav—That's true?

Nimal—Yes, and so you read. But don't leave your play in the middle. I will be your audience.

Manav—Until I don't complete it, I can't say that I will. I feel I would need to be in the mountains for this. It's hard to put it together here.

Nirmal—I remember what Ramakrishna Paramhansa said: 'Rivers can flow because their father—the mountains—are fixed.'

And so, I stand with one and flow with another. And here I go.

And Nirmal Verma left. I started saving money for the mountains.

While writing the play *Colourblind* (my twelfth play), I kept a record of the changes. As I changed, the play changed too. This is a recollection of that process:

. . .

Why do we like a particular painting? When a part of our life resonates with a few colours, we start communicating through them. And we say that we like the painting a lot. I see Rabindranath in colour now. These are thick strokes on a canvas. If I move away, I begin to see spaces in between. These spaces have faces in them. So, I look at the space and the faces and make my way back to the painting only to find a big red mark—as if someone had written the letter 'A' on a blank sheet of paper. I start talking with these strange shapes. I touch the colours; they are still wet. I notice that some colours are missing here. And there's something more that's missing as well. The emptiness . . . it feels like an empty chair; as if someone will come and sit there one day. The thought makes me like the painting more.

After finishing my part in the play *Tagore*, I am drinking chai. I have never done something like this before. To write while remembering a person's life and his words. I felt it was impossible to string together so many scattered pieces. It is a kind of short story that has Rabindranath's presence. But he is nowhere to be seen. It felt like my house had lost many things when I finished writing. It was spacious. The sound was echoing from the corners. The songs I'm singing are also coming back to me. What a hoarse voice! I felt embarrassed and stopped singing. I walk around the house, and I feel so light. I don't even feel the weight of my clothes on my body. The only consolation is chai, which tastes good. The ginger is good for my throat.

. . .

Yesterday was the first time we started experimenting with the initial scenes. Every time, it seemed like we were talking about someone who was there and watching us silently. I've been engrossed in Tagore's life these past few months. It almost felt like he lived in a cottage on a mountain, and every day, with a notebook in hand, I went to meet him. He talked about his life in such a way as if he was talking about his poems. I noted a few things and let go of others. The things I left followed me to the rehearsal space, and the things I wrote seemed useless.

I miss my *nani* (maternal grandmother) very often. Every time I would visit her in her room, I felt that she wanted to say something to me. As we talked, she would suddenly hold my hand tightly in hers. I would stop speaking. She would look at me silently . . . and something would happen. I haven't been able to grasp what happened at that moment. This is how I feel about Tagore. It's as if someone silences me in the middle of a conversation. Something happens, and I miss it. What happens in silence? Why do I miss it? Can I include this sense of missing in the play? I begin to see a story, which follows a traditional route. It is dependable. But all I can think of is my nani's old, wrinkled hand. I can't stop myself from doing that. There is an error between these words, and even if I can see it on a fine day, I never catch it. I want to direct this error. I want to involve her hand, the silence, Tagore and this unnamed 'thing' between us to play out on the stage.

I think a lot about where Tagore is in all of this. Where is the Tagore that everyone knows about? Can I bring him on stage? Can I even describe him? Even just a little? Maybe not. But I have seen it appear in the middle of conversations. I have felt him while reading his work. I felt that at one point, I was like him. So, in the end, even if a glimpse appears on the stage, it would be as close as I could get. I cannot separate myself now. This process has engulfed my eating and drinking, sitting down and then sitting again, getting up, pain, wounds, imbalances, silences, everything. A man who hangs between joy and fear is sitting with me right now. We are drinking chai. '*Kopalein phir phoot aayi hain shaakhon par . . . kahna use . . .* [tell her . . . the buds have sprouted on the branches again].' I read this last night and am still not out of it.

. . .

Tagore. What is in this name? Why am I so drawn to this child? The silence he holds. The way he plays alone. Tagore!

A little child is sitting in a palanquin and begins to live his small life in the middle of a vast playground. He is punished for dipping his head into water at the centre of a chalk pit made by a potter. He watches his father as if he's looking at a film. I don't feel anything is missing in this world. Even Tagore grasped this beauty when he got older. When he was little, he played a lot. When he grew older, he waited—for someone. There was someone who had not yet arrived. Or was it Ratan (the postmaster's daughter) for whom he kept on circling the post office? How does one reach his mental state when one reads his writing? His love is not complete without pain, it seems. When one goes to find pain, one finds love. As a child, he was trying to prove, 'I also exist.' He found Bengal waiting for him when he stepped out to prove himself. When he stepped out of Bengal, the whole country greeted him with open arms. And finally, the whole world acknowledged him. This struggle made him feel small again. And then, he returned to his search—for someone—for that one person. He started circling the post office again. To find the one who would listen to everything he has to say. Then he seemed selfish. He wrote off other people's lives. Not even a single story ended naturally. But the word natural and Tagore don't go together. The amount of work he did in his lifetime was not natural.

There are so many times when I want to talk to him. To enquire—why was he writing so much? What was this constant being of Tagore that made him not want to be Tagore in the end? The burden of all this work—nothing normal in his life.

When I woke up this morning, I felt Tagore was looking at me. He was about to answer my questions. The alarm was blaring. I ran and switched it off and went to bed again. I closed my eyes tightly. I wanted to remember the last glimpses of him. It was all a waste. I kept turning and tossing and finally got up. I put the water on the stove for chai but forgot to turn it on. I kept standing there. I couldn't understand my dream. I had met Tagore (in my dream) when I was living in Switzerland, and he was living there too, waiting for Victoria. But she never came. I was talking to him incessantly, but he was silent. He would sigh, and then everything went quiet. All my questions seemed a waste because I didn't know if he was listening to me or not. Then I realized that I was standing in front of a screen. I was looking at him on a screen.

I turned on the stove. I had started making chai, but I wasn't fully present. I was restless. I had a beautiful image of Tagore in my head. Then suddenly, his waiting disturbed me, and I had the urge to talk to him about it. But he was on screen, and I tried to talk to him but couldn't. After this, he came closer to me. As a human who needed another human at that time, I felt I understood him a little more. Maybe this time, I could hold him while reading his stories or poems, but he slipped away again. Suddenly, I felt that he was there in front of me, looking me in the eye. And then my dream ended. There are moments when we turn weak and lose control. After that, we lose all our meaning because we get busy deciding whether to do something or not. In those moments, we get a chance to see ourselves clearly—naked and without a mirror. Everything lies bare, as it is in front of us, and we are clueless.

Helplessness is the word that connects me to Tagore. I am trying to find poetry in this form in the play.

. . .

There is a screen between Tagore and me. I can never see him fully. I see a man cross the screen to approach me. No, it's not Tagore. He is wearing jeans and a t-shirt. Then he says that he can act like Tagore. I do not hear the word act and start looking for Tagore in him. I ask him to sing, and he starts reciting a poem. I ask him to sit, and he starts dancing. I hear words in his silence, and when he speaks, everything becomes foggy. Who is Tagore? What does being Tagore mean? Do I even understand, or am I only trying to untangle my problems—that which I call Tagore? I always take shelter in my play whenever I am struggling. By the time I resolve my play, my life's worries start to seem worthless. I am going through a deep depression, and only I know about this. There is no shadow of it in my play. I am happy about that.

Whenever I got out for chai and a smoke after rehearsal, I felt a sense of wonderment accompany me. I must hold my breath to feel its presence. It's just as if a butterfly sits on your shoulder; you cannot turn to look at it. The moment you move, it will fly away. I don't know if I'll ever be able to see Tagore fully. Between what I consider wonder and what I think Tagore is, a butterfly breathes. This colourful creature is right in front of me, and I, like a colourblind person, am searching for something. What is witnessing me and what I notice holds a space for the birth of a play. I think about seeing a tomato plant in Kashmir amid this. For some reason, I always thought that tomatoes were manufactured in a market. It was beautiful for me to see them growing on plants. I begin to laugh and then take a few sips of chai, putting out my cigarette. Something resolves inside me, and I repeat Virginia Woolf, 'Let's take a walk.'

. . .

It is lovely to catch a glimpse of life in the moment when lifeless words on paper start breathing. How beautiful it is to see a play take on a life of its own. These ragged first breaths are the pleasure that is called theatre. I think I've found the answer to the simple difference between a play and a film, just now, while witnessing the birth of this play. To see a play being born heals things you thought were dead inside you. This happens only in theatre because a play does not occur in a single day. It is in the continuous gradual birth with every day, every *taleem* (Marathi word for rehearsal, and I like it a lot).

The entire day is spent waiting. I want to see what will happen during rehearsal tonight; I might witness something new. When a sculptor puts her hand in the water and starts touching the clay, something new is born in the world. As for me, the process of writing a play is a little different. I like to sit in front of the pile of clay and look at it for a long time. After a lot of patience, it starts talking to me. It comes alive in parts. I have never been able to decipher when that happens, but my hands rise and start giving shape to it. But it is not I who shapes it; it is the mud that shapes me. I show up—empty and without any thoughts. That is why we accept each other immediately. I don't push my values on her; it doesn't dry up waiting. Whenever such closeness starts developing, I start reminiscing about my childhood and the games we used to play. Right now, we're not there yet. My play is still beginning to breathe under a peepul tree.

. . .

We performed the play *Colourblind* in Kolkata in 2013. After a long struggle, we had all come a little closer to Tagore. We were apprehensive when we had started the show. But with every show, we attained a new meaning for ourselves. I could see it in everyone who was a part of it. This was a challenging play for everyone. Some plays support us before we dive into a difficult phase of life. It's strange to think that these are the final shows of the play. It will only remain in our memories from now on.

I like this thing about theatre. Whatever we create sooner or later gets finished—like life. Theatre is a very momentary art. It remains till it's being played. It's like the way we live. We live in almost the same way every day, but every day is different from the other. Every show is just like that—similar but different from the previous one. There is always some change that takes place when a sculpture gets completed. This change is felt in the maker and the thing that is built. So, we change. And I hope that everyone involved in this play and those who watched it have felt that change.

I saw Tagore walking into my house when I created him in *Colourblind*. We would often pass each other by. He with his silence, I with a heaviness. We made sure not to enter each other's personal space. The day I completed the play and returned home, he got up and left. As he looked at me for the last time, I knew something inside me had died. I can say that I knew Tagore. We had lived together. And then, one day, he left and left nothing behind.

I blew out the lamp of *Colourblind* that I had lit, and realized it was already morning.

Our gatherings mostly ended with poetry. At one time, my friends always asked me to read Bhavani Prasad Mishra's poem, and almost always, I read *Ghar ki Yaad* (The Memory of Home). Most of us were living away from our homes for years. The poem touched people deeply. As its narration ended, everybody would be lost in thoughts, in their own space. Then somebody would joke awkwardly and force people to return from their brooding. Such is Bhavani bhai's writing.

My relationship with Bhavani bhai is old. I had no idea about its existence for a long time. There was an old peepul tree behind the dilapidated fort of Hoshangshah Gauri. My friends and I skipped classes and used it as a hiding place. Soon, our Hindi teacher came to know about it and caught us red-handed. He started thrashing us and then suddenly stopped to say, 'This was the place where Bhavani Prasad Mishra wrote *Sannata* and look at you, you've turned it into filth', and he continued beating us.

When I got up after the beating, I was astonished to have learnt about this. I had never understood poems before. Poets lived in books for me and talked about absurd things. I hated poetry. But this painful experience didn't stop us; we started visiting that place even more frequently. While sitting under the same tree, I opened the poem one day. I saw the bank where the madman used to sit and sing. I heard the queen's sad sighs. The owl, snake and chameleon all were present there. Then I recited the poem to my friends. It was the first time that a poem had made sense to us. Then *Satpuda ke Jungle* naturally made its way into our lives. But even then, poetry had not influenced me, and all of this disappeared as I grew up.

Then I started a relationship with theatre. I came to Bombay and started working as an actor with Satyadev Dubey. I played the lead role in his first play called *Inshah Allah*. At the end of the play, I would recite a poem. I loved it. I used to wait for the play to end to recite *Geet Farosh*. Dubey ji also used to narrate that poem a lot. When I asked him, he said that Bhavani bhai wrote this poem. I thought that Bhavani bhai and Bhavani Prasad Mishra were two different people. I thought Bhavani bhai must be one of his friends (and he was his friend). And it could have been my small-mindedness too. How can a poem written in a small town under an old tree be worthy of being recited in a play in Bombay?

The play was a hit, and we had a party afterwards. Amrish Puri also attended it. All of us young actors were sitting in a corner. I stood up to use the washroom. I was inside when suddenly everything fell silent. Then suddenly, I heard Amrish Puri's resonant voice: '*Toh pehle apna naam bata du du/Phir chupke chupke dhaam bata du tumko/Tum chaunk nahi padna/Yadi dheeme dheeme main apna koi kaam bata du tumko* [I will tell you my name first/Then slowly I will tell you about my place/Don't be shocked if slowly I tell you about the help I need from you].'

I jumped. It was my village, tree and ruins of the fort; everything was mine. Whatever was happening outside belonged to me. I was sitting in the bathroom, trying to hold on to my excitement. The moment the poem ended, everyone started applauding. I came out. I wanted to tell everyone that it was my poem. Bhavani Prasad Mishra wrote this poem while sitting at my favourite spot. I felt that nobody could understand that poem until they saw how the bank looked from under my tree and how the fort stood in the background. How can anyone understand this poem without understanding the spot where I used to sit? My spot. This is my poem. I have been to the same place where it was written. I wanted to say so much, but I was terrified. So, I remained silent. Then everybody started praising Bhavani bhai, and it was then I realized that Bhavani bhai was Bhavani Prasad Mishra. From then on, he became Bhavani bhai for me. He had stepped out of the schoolbook, and we had started a relationship. I told my friends sitting in the corner that this poem was written at my favourite spot. Everybody laughed, but nobody believed me.

In a few years, I had formed a friendship with Dubey ji. My fears of living in small towns had started receding. Dubey ji became lonely as he aged. He would sit at Holiday Inn in the night. I accompanied him on a few of these occasions. We often talked about Bhavani bhai. He said that Bhavani bhai's wife used to get very irritated with him. And when he started writing songs for films, every poet in the country was angry with him. At that time, he wrote *Geet Farosh*. It was his answer to each one of those people. I liked that a lot. I used to read poems to girls and impress them. I knew *Geet Farosh* by heart, and now I even had a story to accompany it. I got very close to Bhavani bhai. The poem that had me fall in love with him was *Sukh ka Dukh*. I had heard this poem from Dubey ji. '*Zindagi mein koi bada sukh nahi hai, is baat ka mujhe bada dukh nahi hai* [That there is no big happiness in life, is not a big deal].' Each word of this poem got under my skin. I said to Dubey ji that I wanted this poem. He said you would use it to flirt with girls. And said no. I tried very hard, but he didn't budge. Then I struggled to find that poem but failed. In the end, one of my friends downloaded it from the internet and gave it to me. I quickly learnt it by heart. I thought I would surprise Dubey ji by reciting it in front of him. But Dubey ji was very sick at that time.

I met him at Prithvi Theatre one day. It was unbearable to see his condition. We both were silently sipping our chai. Then he said, recite a poem for me. The relationship of poetry between us was very sacred. I asked him, 'Bhavani bhai?' and he smiled in reply. The poem that I had wanted to recite—I didn't. Instead, I recited, '*Aaram se bhai zindagi zara aaram se/tezi tumhare pyar kee bardasht nahin hoti ab/ itna kaskar kiya gaya alingan zara zyada hai/ jarjar is shareer ko/araam se bhai zindagi zara araam se* [Do it with ease life, do it with ease/I can't tolerate your force now/this tight embrace is too strong/ to a broken body/ Do it with ease life, do it with ease].' He kept listening to me with rapt attention. He was amazed that he didn't know about this one. He asked me for this poem. I said he should give me *Sukh ka Dukh* first. He started laughing and said, 'I will never give you that poem.' I didn't tell him that I already had it. Then I said I would give it to him the next time we met. But I couldn't keep my promise, for he was admitted to the hospital soon after this, and after being in a coma for three weeks, he passed away.

When some of his closest friends gathered in Prithvi to pay their homage, I was asked to read a poem. I took out *Sukh ka Dukh* from my pocket. I wanted to talk about my whole journey to this poem. I wanted to talk about the journey from Bhavani Prasad Mishra to Bhavani bhai. I wanted to tell them about the fort in ruins, the tree where I sat down and read the poem to my friends for the first time. I wanted to tell the whole story from *Aaram se Bhai Zindagi Zara Aaram Se* to *Sukh ka Dukh* and then read the poem because once you know the story behind the poem, it becomes yours. But I didn't do that. I read the poem. And left the place. I'd come close to Bhavani bhai because of Dubey ji and grew closer to Dubey ji because of Bhavani bhai. There are very few writers who make you want to spend an evening with them. To think about taking a walk together. To listen to them recite their poems and then ask, 'Did you write *sannata* [silence] sitting under the old peepul tree?'

Shows for *Red Sparrow* (my tenth play) have ended. Many people loved it while others didn't get it. The play was challenging to write for me. The actors and I had a lot of fun on stage. In the after-play gatherings, I met many people. They all put forward their understanding of it. I agreed with them all. They all had their place from where they saw the play. When I returned home afterwards, I felt satisfied. An experiment that took shape in my mind had manifested the same way. I had only one thought—celebrating *Red Sparrow*.

It was a few conversations with writers, some discussions between writers, characters debating among themselves and their relationships with each other. I wanted to celebrate this writing, where all the writers are heroes or a character. It was made in the style of a thriller and a comic book. My direction was influenced a little by Bukowski. It was infused with plenty of small connections that had pleased me while writing it. I think the actors felt them while performing.

You create the world you live in; I have read that somewhere. I want to extend this thought. I have created a world—of plays, stories and writing. I live in that world. Those who come close to me witness whatever lies in this world. What I write makes me who I am . . . nothing exists outside.

I tried not to tell a story in this play. I have wanted to do this for a very long time. Both *Park* and *Red Sparrow* seemed to have achieved that to some extent.

There's a tree in front of my house. Many birds, like kingfishers, sparrows, parakeets, crows, cranes, kites and owls, sit on it, completely unaware that the world is changing. Sometimes I yell in their direction, 'The world is coming to an end. Why don't you care, friends?' But they don't even look at me. These 'poor ones' don't even know what's happening. I look at them in pity. By 2050 the country will be taken over by Maoists, I tell the birds on my windowsill. Some people would still want to create a society they read of in books, while others would turn everyone into a Hindu, Muslim or Christian. Some will be forced to die only because of language, some for the colour of their skin, others for caste while killing for religion is happening even now. Listening to this, some cranes flew away, and one little bird flew into my balcony. I told her, 'Listen, you little bird and tell this to your friends too. Your skill of flying away at loud sounds will not save you anymore. You will have to learn something new. First, you'll have to find people like me who consider you unfortunate. Then don't fly so proudly. You'll have to fly like you are unfortunate. If people don't pity you, your survival in this society as civilized as this is difficult.' The bird turned its head in a different direction. I think it got angry at me. So, I made my voice softer and said, 'I think you don't know this, but humans have started searching for beings like you. They are finding out everything about you . . . colour, language, caste, everything. But if you pretend to be unfortunate and become an endangered species, then maybe they will care.' On the last line, it flew away. 'She will also die,' I shrugged.

After a while, I noticed two birds sitting on my balcony. I think one of them was the bird I was talking to before. Maybe my speech was too complex for her, and now she'd brought her friend, who might be more intelligent. Or perhaps I was not able to explain it fully. I said again, 'Listen, I am not able to say it fully, but it's only human not to be able to.' I liked this sentence. So, I went with it, 'See. People can never exactly say what they want to say. The world that some people have imagined is said to be wonderful. A man thought about such an ideal world and wrote about it. Some people even believed that if the world looked so beautiful in the book it would be more beautiful in reality. Then these people tried to convince others but failed. And now there are a lot of such books. People like to collect them. The world looks spectacular in them. So, they say. Now, people want to create this imaginary world as soon as possible. And they have decided to kill those who don't want to be part of their version of the world' The two birds pooped. They looked at me one last time and flew away. I started shouting, 'So, you think I'm joking? You wait until it happens. One way or the other, the world will change. Either Hindus will kill everyone and paint the country saffron, or Islam will swallow everybody. Maybe Maoists will control us and try to create an ideal society, or Christianity will compel people to confess their sins. The world will not stay the same. So, listen, you puny birds, try to look as helpless as possible if you want to stay alive. In a storm of change, it will be the weak who will survive. So better start working on it.'

We used to spend our afternoons sitting on our doorsteps. A world of stories was created over chai. A thin veil separated home and the world. While playing, I would venture outside again and again only to return home.

Now I keep the word 'return' safe in my pocket. Whenever it drops out, I look at it and remember my old home's doorstep. Is a return even possible?

Whenever we go back to where we used to live, it doesn't feel like we returned to the same place. When we touch the door, a splinter pokes our fingers. The thin veil-like curtain has gone. While earlier we used to run from door to door now our head bangs into the door frame while entering. And we sit down in pain; the memories of those afternoons return. And we begin missing our home while sitting in it. This return is still safe in our pockets. It's become an old monochrome picture from our childhood.

. . .

Didn't it all start with a delicate dream? We were not used to handling such tenderness, so we buried it deep inside. We were afraid that people would make fun of it, so we crushed the seed. And when it finally sprouted, it wasn't green. The colour seemed more like my mother's old sarees, of her love, the old walls of our home, the streets of my village, the snow in Kashmir and the sky.

This sapling smelled of all that I couldn't live through. There were no flowers. It would take a lot of time for that. These were still the tender roots that were waiting for a good rain.

In her village, she had a hiding place where she went to dream her big dreams. They sparkled in the sky like a star. Although she couldn't say it to anyone, she knew this was the thing she had been searching for all her life. Looking at it, she would fall asleep in the courtyard. When the sun in the morning woke her up, everything looked as it was. But she couldn't see her star. Could she only see it as a dream? Was it not real? She wasn't ready to accept it.

So, she wove a bridge from the hidden star to the morning light. She ran on that bridge and jumped. The dream's fulfilment holds a river, trust, a bird and a look—she has become the star.

I look for a kite whenever I look at the sky. Kites have my childhood preserved in them. When we were in Kashmir, and I walked the streets with my father, I talked about having a nightmare. Then someone would say that you should tell your dream to the kite. It will spread it across the sky, and it will never return. I didn't believe it. So, he said, you must assume. Like in mathematics, every problem begins with 'let's assume'. So 'let us assume' that the kite is listening to your dreams. Or let's assume that I am not with you.

I assumed that my father was not with me on this street in Srinagar. I wasn't ready for it. We are never prepared for our people to disappear. I got restless and said, 'Let's assume this is all a dream.' Suddenly, a kite came flying and landed in front of me. What was this? I told the kite that I did not want this dream. Wake me up from this sleep. Where is my papa? There is so much to do. The kite flew after hearing all this. I stood there for a long time and whispered, 'Let's assume I was a good son.'

I want to get lost. Ruin everything and start all over again. When I know that turning in this direction would mean no return, I acknowledge the pain involved and take it. I know that I am a normal human being, yet I get attracted to that which is different. In all of it, I wear a cloak of 'I am a good person'. When I get lost on the way, I feel that these roads have tricked me. After all, I was a good person. But deep inside, there's a satisfaction in being deceived. When everything I've made starts to crumble, I run towards 'I am a good person'. But I get late—every time. I get tired right before complete defeat.

I understand what goes on between the sun and the sunflower right before it's about to wilt, but I'm late in catching it. Every time I say the reason is you and then forget to look into the mirror.

My brother and I must have been eight or nine when we left Kashmir. The sadness of leaving Kashmir was less than the sadness of leaving Titli. She was our first love. While leaving, I couldn't stop myself and broke down before her. My brother came and said coolly, 'Let's go' and asked for one of her monochrome pictures. I had laughed at my brother's stupidity at that time. I had explained what true love is. But very soon, I realized it was I who was a fool.

We had left Kashmir and now talked about it only in stories. But whenever we did, we remembered Titli. My brother would leave and go to the other room. I knew that he was looking at her monochrome photograph. For years to come, I would regret breaking down in front of her. It took a lot of effort to make him show me her photograph. I had to make him happy before he let me look. I was not allowed to stare at her or touch the photograph. She looked like a fairy. It seemed like she would come out of the picture and give me wings to fly. The photograph didn't stay with my brother for long. We were now roaming the streets of our village. Titli had disappeared.

My father was on his last trip to Kashmir a few years ago, where he happened to meet Titli's family. When he returned home, we both asked at once, 'How is she?'

He replied, 'She got married, and while giving birth to her first child, her legs got paralyzed. Her husband left her. She was depressed. She died some time back.'

We brothers didn't want to know any further. After a long silence, my brother got up and went inside his room. I knew he would be looking at her photograph. But this time, I couldn't stop myself and went after him. I was about to open the door when I heard his voice. He whispered, 'Titli'. Scared, I peeked in. There he was, an inch above the ground; my brother was floating in the air.

I know this fragrance. It courses through my veins. When I am near my mother, the whiff comes in the happiest moments. This fragrance is like Kashmir—my Kashmir. But this is not the Kashmir that we talk about on TV or discuss in meetings. It is the smoke leaving from a bakery early in the morning, the smell of the freshly baked bread; it is kahwa, a kite, Khawajabad, Abdulla's tonga, it is the Bukhari, Titli, Feran, Banihal, rajma chawal. It is the open sky with soft white clouds. But these clouds do not form the shapes of elephants or horses. These are the clouds in the aftermath of an explosion. They do not carry rain; they have stories. Stories that are like sunlight after snow. Believe me when I say, my Kashmir is very different from the Kashmir that you know about. It is a place with a fragrance that comes from my navel in the most beautiful moments.

It had become a habit to talk to the river. I spent many afternoons sitting on the banks of the river Narmada. It comforted me to think that the river could take everything I told her. There would be a long tunnel, like the Jawahar tunnel, with light at the end. In that light, everything would look as it is. The word 'I' would dissolve in that light, and everyone would talk in 'us'. Every complex thing would start sounding simple. And that relief, in the end, would make me free, and one day, when I could put that freedom in the river and watch it float away, that would be the day when I forgive myself.

At some point in life, it felt like we were Godot. We struggled to reach the place where people were waiting for us. The journey seemed haphazard; we were restless. And because we were troubled, we didn't forget to trouble others. It felt like things would be okay once we reached that place. That place where they will say, 'Oh! Here you are. We've been waiting for you for so long!' But then, almost suddenly, we stopped. We realized that we were the people who were waiting, and it was somebody else who was Godot. We started making excuses for our passiveness, reciting Buddha's teachings. But even then, we didn't see Godot. So, we resolved to walk. When we reached the end of our strength and were thoroughly exhausted, we saw a place that was more beautiful than anything we had imagined. Suddenly, our destination and the waiting seemed of no use. Words such as carelessness, wonder, aimlessness and curiosity seemed more attractive. It was good that Godot didn't arrive; what would we do with him? And it was also good that we weren't him and didn't wander. And now the situation is such that if I happen to see Godot in this journey, I wouldn't recognize him, and if someone calls out 'Godot', I wouldn't remember to answer.

How long does it take to jump? I have seen fear floating in places where people never dared to dive in. It is not the water that drowns us but the fear of what comes next. It is tragic to talk about swimming without entering the waters. We are but a story. And in the span of a few hundred years, our story would be insignificant. So, what are we afraid of? Why do we look for our story in someone else's life? In truth, we can never win in our story; we can only live it. Silence is the room where we pray. It is the place where the story gets interesting. If we try to decorate this room with ornaments, we will kill its sanctity. But alas! We have a habit of improving our homes, and we put things in them that resemble what we once wanted in life. And that is how the story becomes boring.

At one time in my life, I dreamed a lot about bridges. People had created a fear that it's all lost if one crosses a bridge. There is no return once you're on the other side. My childhood was filled with sights of trains and bridges. Where do they carry these people? What lies beyond this thing I should be afraid of? And then, one day, I stepped on a bridge. It was empty, and I was barefoot. The sun was up in the sky, my shadow right underneath me. I know I wasn't dreaming.

I guess they were right when they said there is no return. I got lost and stopped caring about my return. Now, I often pinch myself, wondering if it's all a dream.

Nobody ever thought that one day she'd get up and leave. Leave the trade of being a good girl that had been hers forever. But she did. All the good girls and women were left behind without customers. All they could do was watch her leave.

Although there were no visitors anymore, these women would open their shops every morning out of habit. They had one more thing to do along with this opening and closing. During the day, they would pretend to visit each other and start talking about her. They soon concluded that her departure had been a big mistake. And they took pride in staying behind.

A long time passed. The one who had run away was called a bird because whenever they talked about her, they inevitably looked at the sky. And the village was called a well where all the good women had the same language. You can still hear it. It goes something like, 'ribbit . . . ribbit', by order!

This happens every time it rains. To have a cup of chai and then look outside the window. In truth, rain brings a lot with itself—old windows, balconies, a shirt with broken buttons, one sock, moments of a soft touch, staying up all night and the fragrance of home. And we sigh coldly. An old tune plays in a house, and it feels like old photographs have come alive and are sitting on the windowsill. The song changes, and so does the colour of the window. The rain doesn't take anything away. It collects it. We can only have chai and witness the changing of our windows.

To witness rain is to be soaking wet in it.

The sadness of a person's death is less than the grief of losing the relationship that you shared with them. You feel betrayed. As if there was a bridge and you both had agreed to walk on it from your ends. You had named the bridge your relationship. Suddenly, that person disconnected and left. And now you stand on the edge of this half-bridge. You can see their life from here, but you will never fully know it. And every day it will disappear more and more.

Very slowly, we have crawled into this point in time. We have become something like humans after many permutations and combinations. We all share a common state of alertness now. There is a fear of and from this alertness. This fear gives birth to several rules. And then it starts attracting other concerns. When we look at the rules created by fear, more fears cling to us. And we begin calling them the rules of living. The fear of caution lies far away, and we start to live in the reflections of fear. Then the rules of fear become the rules of God. The tragedy begins when we start fighting for these rules. There are no rituals or traditions to fighting. It has its own rules, fears and reflections. Once it begins, it ends only when everything is destroyed.

Sometimes strange things make me feel like, 'Oh! It's just like me.' Like a computer—no, not the new ones, but the old models. I think I am an old computer. Look how I stop working whenever a lot is going on! When I go to a beautiful place, I always wonder if I have the space to store such wonder on my hard drive. I pick up very little—only as much as I can handle. I know I will stop working if I take more. I work on an ancient operating system. It has its advantages. Like, when there's a lot of pain, it stops bothering me. It gets easy by itself as time goes by. Similarly, helplessness seeps in so slowly that it becomes a part of my life, and I don't even notice. Sometimes if you ask for chai, it's not me but the helplessness that answers.

There was an old game on an old computer: Pacman. I am like him. I try to eat up all the good that hides underneath the avalanche of sadness.

Some houses from my childhood were left behind. I always felt they had not been destroyed. And that one day I will return. But can we ever go back to the same place? And then comes a time when thoughts start forcing themselves on our dreams, and we know it's time.

Twenty-six years later, when he returned, everything had changed. He stood in the courtyard of the house for a long time—the place which was his home. Memories of the past started seeping out from the same cracks he used to stock up his candies in. The door was locked. He looked through the cracks. Ghosts of his past were dancing in the ruins. The stickers he put on the wooden cupboard were still there—Bruce Lee, Nag Raj, Chacha Chaudhary, Phantom, Billu and Pinki. He tried to push the door open, but the rusted lock stopped him. The key was stashed away somewhere in his new house. He felt it was time he stashed away his childhood with it too. Some things could now only be seen through the cracks of old broken homes.

One morning, long after he had returned to the city, he woke up suddenly. He saw himself standing at the foot of his bed. It was as if he was watching a silent movie in front of the ruins of his past. The corners of the bed were dripping with tales of years gone by. And yet, he got up, trying to gather all the pieces he'd lost along the way. He felt if only he could go back to the place where he was about to sprout—germinate from the ground to become a tree, he could get it all back. That moment held all the answers. He wanders now, and when he returns home, he finds himself standing at the foot of his bed again. The way he stood in front of his broken-down house.

. . .

Then I thought I should just purge it, maybe tell somebody who'll understand about it. Or maybe just write it down or put it in a book and then throw it into the river or maybe lose it in a game. I tried everything when it appeared for the first time. I knew this dream would not go away quickly. It is like a sore that doesn't let you sleep. It's like a story that begs to be finished. And when I reached a point and sighed with relief, thinking it was the end, a narrow lane popped up. It is connected to roads and roads of possibilities. The dream had begun when I thought of 'taming the untamable'. The entire sky is untamable. This morning is untamable. And it seems like I'm back to the first day when it appeared. Can I call you my first day?

'I can't sleep.' She used to become quiet after saying this. Her eyes would gaze in the distance when she talked about books. She asked why most books talk about men and why everything seems so tangled, like the strings of kites. Then she would climb on top of the terrace like a child and stare at the sun, 'Is my life my own, or does it belong to somebody else's story? Why are we more present in other people's stories than our own? Can we bring ourselves back?'

A wise man's deep, experienced voice comes from somewhere, 'To try to untangle it is to tangle it forever'.

'Interesting,' she chuckles, 'I will try to untangle it then.'

'But why?'

'Because these strings are mine. Shouldn't I be the one who decides what happens to them?' A little girl gets busy untangling the strings in the sun, and suddenly, all the men grow afraid.

When I was young, I always carried an umbrella when it rained. This umbrella was like always having my schoolmaster with me. I yearned to step into the rain and forget that he was watching. But I was afraid of the scolding and so stayed under my umbrella. I would curse it and feel angry. Then I learnt to deceive it. I devised plans to leave the umbrella at home and started getting drenched in the rain. I just wanted it so bad that all the umbrellas in the world didn't matter anymore.

Nowadays, there is no schoolmaster following me around. I prefer staying inside and watching the rain from my window. When I step out of my house, it's not the umbrella I forget but to get drenched.

Age seems to have caught up more with our parents when we see them after a long time. Their hands, shoulders, necks and especially the shadows underneath the eyes seem to have changed. Seeing all this, the filial duty cries, 'I will take care of you.' I want to nurture and scrub away the darkness under their eyes. But it turns out we cannot scrub away things, especially the darkness. But we do hurt ourselves and others in the struggle.

Everything eases and starts flowing swiftly once we surrender. Amidst all this, when I see a flock of birds flying away, I never know whether I like them better flying away or staying on the tree.

We will kill everyone who is not like us.

If we want to live like this, then there are reasons aplenty. It is almost like meeting someone who has the same old story that goes something like, 'My father was such a good man. It was the relatives who turned out to be cunning.' I have never met someone who said that he or his father was that villain in the story. So, let's do one thing. Let us kill all the bad guys. Then the only people left would be the heroes. But the problem is that all of them, Hindus, Muslims, Sikhs or Christians, are heroes in their versions of the story. We are each other's relatives. We have played a part in millions of stories for thousands of years. So, does that mean we can uproot each other's stories and kill everybody? Indeed.

And if such a thing happens and only the heroes remain, the world would indeed be too dull a place to live in. I'd prefer a happy death.

Aeroplanes seemed different, foreign; trains, familiar, my own. The whistle blows as cheerfully as a chai is poured into small earthen cups. Trains could take us to our destination in the future. And if we missed one, the cross at its back would console us that this journey was not meant for us. And soon, our train would arrive. Our first long journey was on a train. Jhelum Express and the Punjab Mail are two important trains for me. The rhythm of the train feels like my mother's heartbeat. Whenever I travel on it, I sleep like a baby.

I don't know how many people have given in after struggling with darkness. There is no telling when the fighting becomes intoxicating, and taking lives becomes a pleasure. There are many reasons why people have become accustomed to the dark. Those who have crossed it know how painful it can be, almost as if the skin is peeling off your bones. There was a light shining like hope at the end of the tunnel. With no space to run, we started to crawl. While some took refuge in the darkness and made it their home, planting their legacy, religion and lineage in it, others kept on crawling. Only those with patience made it to the end. Patience—not to wait for the victory of light over dark but to value the darkness and digest the brightness of the light.

When he looked up at the sky, he felt that someone watched over him in the most challenging of times. It was not the sky but the white clouds that had a comforting familiarity; he could see faces. There was someone who saved him before he fell. Someone sent sweet dreams his way so that he didn't get lost. Someone that silently floated like a fragrance in the air. This is the reason why he never got scared before leaping. He jumped, fell and got up. As soon as he was up, he looked at the sky . . . he saw it again; maybe it was the friend who passed away too soon or the girl he loved who died in an accident or maybe his grandmother or his father who, he thought, would never leave him. Whenever he saw a kite gliding between the clouds under a clear blue sky, he felt it was a sign, and he took the next leap. The sky was as big and as dependable as his father.

The earth was an open field,
Where green grass and trees flourished.
People played and had fun,
and everything was good.
Then friends grew,
Relationships too
And we started calling each other family.
Families had wishes;
Wishes wanted houses;
Our houses claimed walls and roofs.
The games changed
And we made rules.
Soon people won or lost.
The ones losing became demons.
Those who won
Became gods.
Demons were banished
And gods gained more spaces,
Which were named later on.
Some were temples; some were churches
And others were called mosques.
Then a voice commanded that everyone was wrong;

Only our game is right
And only our victory pure.
Our god is the 'one'.
And thus began the fight.
Everyone forgot it was just a game
And a search for the 'one' began.
This was a new game
And blood coursed.
There was no right or wrong.
There were no demons here.
This game only had gods.
Every god knew the 'truth'.
And you know how the rest of the story goes . . .
One day there will be no houses.
Only ruins will cover the land.
The earth was a field with no boundaries,
countries or demons, had someone said
that person would be brought to court
That person would soon be dead.

It's always a relief to see that the witness of our existence persists in some old picture albums, toys, broken things and mud houses. Even in a state of ruin, they surround us, reminding us of where we came from. I start caressing the scars around my knees and elbows when I see such things. These are like the stories of a childhood well spent. The sadness of growing up is that the hurt is not outside. Some scars can never be healed. Some kinds of pain would never be comforted.

During long, sleepless nights, I see a clean slate. I go out on the balcony as if my sleep lies abandoned there. Abandoned things don't let you sleep, so I sit and look at the moon. Soon, all my life's doings start provoking my anxiety. So, I start remembering the sweeter mornings that are yet to come. In a way, I begin marking on a clean slate, but these are not just marks; these are efforts. I try to draw the first letter of the word sleep. But that letter glitters like the star next to the moon and begins telling another story. I start writing on the slate, but the balcony is not the house. If the home is asleep, then the balcony is its dream.

We all hold secrets. We let our goodness out in the open for everyone to see and hide our shame. So much so that we don't even want to see how we have wiped out entire species of animals and plants to fulfil our needs. We don't even feel strange when animals get scared at the mere sight of us. I had once heard that old trees in the mountains kept your secret if you tell them. They absorb everything, and we are forgiven. But we have chopped down those trees and have turned them into homes that look like graves. And with nowhere to go, we sit with eyes wide open, filled with our shame. Is there any time left? Our claws remind us that we were animals once, but then we quickly eat some bites of religion and fall asleep again.

The people that I meet these days tell me I've started looking like you. The wrinkles on my face resemble yours. A time comes when we start looking like our mothers and fathers, and we don't even realize it.

Nowadays, if I see a chappal lying on top of the other, I quickly fix it. I get up many times at night to check if the lights in the bathroom are turned off. I look for news about Kashmir in the papers. I check my face in the mirror every time I hear the word Baramulla. I stare at the new lines on my face for a long time. I smell the fragrance of Ponds powder on my handkerchief all day long. It feels like the ground beneath my feet is not stable anymore; as if the house remains, but the foundation slips away. I still have your number saved as Papa. Sometimes I dial it and listen to the bell ring for a long time.

'Never get involved in trying to look for reasons,' my mother said softly.

'How can anything be done without it? It would help if you had a reason for doing things,' the son replied with his newfound knowledge.

'Killing time, that's what finding reason is for. You'll get much time to kill when you are old. But right now, do things that you like. Eat and enjoy like a child does. But make sure that you're not full because then you'll start looking for reasons again. Why did you eat? But if you like eating and still stay hungry, then just do that.' Saying, she returned to her book. The son felt his stomach grumble, and he ran to the bathroom.

I bought shoes from Nike's new collection for my mother.

If she'd known how much they cost me, she'd never wear them. In the morning, she looked at them for a long time, then she slipped into her chappals and got ready to head out. 'Where are you going?' I asked.

'For a walk,' she replied.

'So, why don't you put on your new shoes? I asked a bit surprised.

She said that if she wore them, they would get dirty. So, I made her wear them. With much hesitation, she started walking down the stairs. I was standing at the door, looking at her. She looked like a little girl of five or six. She would grab the side rails after every other step. She was afraid.

'What's the matter?' I asked.

She said that the last time she had put on shoes was when she was in school. She never wore shoes after that. I looked at my mother as if I was seeing her for the first time. After a while, I went to the balcony to look at her. She was standing downstairs.

'What happened?' I asked her again.

She said that she was feeling suffocated.

'You will get used to it,' I said.

She began to walk slowly. She wanted to look at her shoes to see how her feet were looking and hence wobbled.

I could not see her walk like that, so I returned to where I was sitting. There is so much we don't know about our parents.

An older woman lives in the house below mine. I see her sitting on the balcony, reading whenever I walk by. Sometimes, through her window, I would see her dancing while relying on her walking stick. It makes me smile. Although she lives on her own, she is always busy doing one thing or the other. I have never seen a hint of sadness on her wrinkled old face.

I often think that her house stores countless stories that always swim in the air. Sometimes, when the floor in my house gets too warm, I wonder if it's the heat that's coming off from the tales that are crumbling away in her house. In the autumn days, I have seen her collecting sticks and leaves. I have wondered: what does she do with them? The floor of my house always becomes warm on days when she does that.

One autumn night, I suddenly woke up from my sleep. I don't know why but I felt the urge to touch the floor. It was colder than usual. I felt uneasy and decided to go downstairs. I peered through her window, and what do I see? Leaves were dancing in the air while she was lying down, not on the floor but much above it. She suddenly looked at me and said, 'I'm thirsty.'

'I'll get you some water,' I replied hurriedly.

'No, not now. You've stopped putting out water for the birds. It keeps me thirsty.'

I pinched myself. I was sure this was a dream. But nothing happened. I nodded and ran back to my house. The following day as I set a bowl of water on my balcony, a bird limped towards it to have a drink from it.

Whenever I lie to myself, I try to look away—looking away from whom? From myself? But where is this 'I' in my body? Wasn't it the 'I' who had lied in the first place? But then, who am I shying away from? Is there another who is living with 'I' inside me? And all this while this 'I' has been hiding from it? I chuckled at the thought, but I didn't want to laugh. So, if it wasn't I who laughed, then who was it? Why does everything become so unstable? Who makes simple things difficult?

I stood in front of the mirror and said, 'I'm sorry. Please forgive me.' I looked at myself after a very long time and saw a shadow underneath my eyes. I have grown old; it's time I start forgiving myself.

Leaving for school on a *tonga* on chilly mornings,
Stealing away a few hours to play during exams,
Finding a dark corner and playhouse there,
Spending summer afternoons at Mumtaz
bhai's eating a fruit named kabeet,
Getting scared to death watching Tadaka die in Ramleela,
Diving deep in the river and finding a ten paisa coin,
Waiting for days for a kachori and a little jalebi,
Dreaming about finding money and
planning how to spend it,
Talking about our God at the Mazar,
Wishing I was clever one day.
Smelling the rain and getting soaked in it,
Learning how to play the banjo but always
dreaming of playing the tabla,
Stepping out of my house with a will to never come back,
Learning how to ride a bike in the scorching heat,
Letting go of peepul and tamarind and looking for a banyan's shade,
Leaving home and then returning every time,

Everything has poetry in it, but it doesn't belong to us. It is
for another. Even the most personal things are not ours to

keep. We may read it after a long time, but deep down, we know who it is for.

In all honesty, life is a letter we write to someone else. When we've lived it all, we want to sit under the sweet shade of a big banyan tree and drink chai. As the soft sun caresses our old hands, we take out the letter and start reading. That person will think that our life is a story, and as we walk through the jungles of these lies, we will live them all one last time.

Come, let's hide—from reasons to be happy, from the mere waiting for things, from the momentum of time, from sleep, from long nights, from all our dreams, fleeting victories or the need to always look fine, from expectations, from running all the time, from weak moments, from mirrors, defeat, or God, from good things, from love for the country, from being a Hindu or a Muslim, from you and I, from a lifetime of love, from getting you or letting you go, from all the crying and making up—come let's hide, from this hiding and the chance of being found.

When difficulties arise, I try to accept them peacefully. It makes me think about times when I have been the cause of someone else's pain. It doesn't take too long before a familiar face shows up. We often hurt the people who are dearest to us. The pain I've caused to these people still burns like a smouldering fire inside me. There was a time when my mother warned me against hurting a person. The pain they feel never leaves without touching you, she would say. I have tried to get rid of that pain, but instead, I walk with my head bowed down in sadness. I do not ask for forgiveness. That is not mine to claim. I try to live through this pain. And through all of this, I pray that I never become the reason for causing such pain to someone else. This prayer gives me relief and inside this relief is a hope that maybe I can forgive myself one day.

It is Diwali today. I can't imagine how important this festival was during our childhood. The schools in Kashmir would be closed for almost two months. Father would buy us plenty of fireworks, and I would cry at the loud sound they made. I always preferred *fuljhari, anar* and the serpent over the noisy ones and loved saving up my stash of these little firecrackers for a long time. In Hoshangabad, I started enjoying *Ramleela* (enacting the story of lord Rama) instead. We did our little street show in the afternoons. There was no audience, but some four or five of us would set up a makeshift stage with dupattas and start enacting the story.

Two boys in our neighbourhood, Raju and Chotu, could recite the complete play by heart. Naturally, one played the protagonist Rama and the other his brother Lakshman. My elder brother became Bharat and, I got the last character— Shatrughan. Shatrughan had no part in the story so I would walk around Rama or Lakshman aimlessly with my bow and arrow. In the evenings, we used to watch the burning of the effigies of Ravana and Kumbhkaran.

My favourite part of the whole day was finding my friends in the marching armies of Rama and Ravana. The fair kids were recruited in Rama's army while the darker in the enemy's. It never occurred to me that the division was made solely based on skin colour. But I feel strange writing about it today. I wonder if the darker children would have been more apt to play Rama's monkeys, now that I think about it.

On the other hand, Ravana was a most learned priest . . . why was his army dark-skinned? This made no sense. And if I saw my friends, I shouted out their names, which would embarrass them. The children who enacted the role of soldiers in Ravana's army were ridiculed while Rama's monkeys were not told anything for the rest of the year. Sometimes I wonder where Hemant, Nikhil, Hemraj, Patwa, Raju, Maneesh, Bunty and Vicky are today? Where has life taken them? They could be dressed in new clothes today and be happy. Nowadays, I get sad when I see fireworks. How insensitive we are! We share this planet with such beautiful animals, birds and trees. How sensitive they are! And yet we choose to blow our bombs and crackers near them. I have grown out of all these festivities. They bore and pain me. I missed eating *pooris*, and so I made some today. They didn't turn out well. But in all this chaos, they seemed like the most apt thing.

I get nervous whenever everything is going well. I become very anxious. What do I do when everything is going well? I have faced most of my difficult days alone, and it always seemed the right thing to do. But what do I do when I'm happy?

I cannot sit still. So, I call up my friends and talk incessantly. Once, one of them asked, 'Are you okay?' and I replied sadly, 'I am very happy.' I was very happy, but the words fell like habitual lies from my mouth. We were silent for some time and then started laughing. When we had bought a new fridge, everyone had a sore throat from the cold water. We had no idea what to do with it. It had taken us months to figure out. All we would do is find excuses for a chance to touch it with our fingers and then clean the smudges quickly with a cloth. Can happiness be touched like that? Can the smudges of fear be cleaned afterwards with a cloth?

The day I told my mother that I was leaving for Bombay, she had laughed.

'What will you do there?'

I had no answer to her question.

She then took my hand in hers and stared at it for some time. I remember it was a cool winter afternoon. We were sitting in the courtyard.

'Oh!' she exclaimed, and I knew I wouldn't like what was to follow. She spoke after a while.

'You don't have any luck line, son; you have many struggles lying ahead.'

I started rubbing my hand, and she laughed, saying, 'Not this struggle; your life requires much hard work. But there is one good thing.'

'What is it?' I jumped at the sight of hope.

'The good thing is that you have labourer's hands.'

A butterfly was sitting on her shoulders, and I wondered if it remembered the time it was a caterpillar. Does a bird check her lines before starting her day to find food?

I shrugged and was gone the following day.

It's not so easy to follow one's heart! So many temptations need to be given up. A lot of dear ones made upset and angry. Some even leave forever. It seems so strange that it is the only life we have, yet it takes so long to grasp it! The mind wants to stay murky like soiled linen, but everyone you meet has a new soap to scrub the dirt off you. They don't let you lose, and the battle of winning becomes endless. Nothing makes sense. But a tree grows where nothing could, and everything becomes meaningful again.

It is easy to be complicated,
But hard to stay easy.
It's easy to feel lonely in a crowd,
But it is difficult to live alone with yourself.
It is easy to talk and difficult to do.
It's as if it's easy to stay up all night
But challenging to have a long, restful sleep.
Like an entire life seems so short
But an evening long.
Like the teacher is sincere
But the student, not.
It is easy to be in pain.
To have no pain is hard.
To hate others is easy,
To love oneself a task.
To drown in love is easy,
To stay afloat difficult.
To write all of this is easy
But to do what I write is not.

Years will pass, and he will fade away. Time will bury him—his broad shoulders, his heavy hands with the tattoo of 'Manohar' on his arms. He will wave at me from a mountaintop one day; I know this. But my being is not ready to accept it right now. I am fighting to keep him intact against the passage of time. The despair now is not about his leaving, but my struggle of keeping him alive. Can't I stop things from happening? I can still feel him touch my forehead. His stubble still pokes at my cheeks. But he is not mine wholly. I only have him in pieces, experiences and memories. It's as if the tree is gone, but the leaves are still scattered on the ground. Can't I collect them and bring them home? Can I bring Kashmir to my home and keep it safe in a cupboard?

We had planted a tree in happier times. In the dark of the night, it stepped into our sleep. As time passed and the plant grew, it began showing up in our lives, in our words and our work. We named the plant a 'dream'. As time passed, we forgot when we had planted its seed. Like the vine of amar-bel, it spread across our lives. So much so that now we have to cut and trim and prune it to find ourselves. It was very late when we realized that our dream had become so massive that we were wilting under it. One day a friend from childhood came to see us. He wasn't a friend actually; he was our childhood. He looked for us in our home but couldn't find us because we were lying unconscious, intoxicated by our dream.

Whenever my mother starts talking about her life, it feels like she's taken out a story from a Tolstoy novel. It starts from anywhere and goes in different directions, talking about many situations and places that it seems like many stories are being narrated simultaneously. There are many tales that we still haven't finished yet. In her stories, the characters she mentions casually have their life's worth of adventures.

Her life was shaken to the ground many times. Whenever she finds herself in a new city, in a new environment, she builds life from scratch all over again. It seems like most of our mothers have had a difficult life.

Suddenly, I feel like I'm standing in front of a tall mountain. I can hear all the sounds, including the birds, eagles, seeds and trees. Everything seems insignificant in front of that giant mountain, especially my collection of sad stories, stubborn nature and the like.

'We are not living in vain.' We have never been able to digest this statement. We have never been able to accept that there is a significant reason behind our existence. All our anger and ego sprout from knowing that one day we will die, and no one will care less about it. But if you look closely, it is a better way to live and does not affect anyone else. You came in softly and left without making a noise. Although you didn't add anything to nature, you also didn't steal anything from it. But we want to live on even after we die. And nature has no interest in it. That is why we want to destroy her. Just as people start throwing rocks at the caged lion, they wanted to be acknowledged for their existence; but the animal couldn't care less.

We are sad and realize later that this sadness has stemmed from the past. We are living the same sadness repeatedly. The smaller pains affect us so much that the bigger ones must wait. They just have to wait outside our door. In sorrow and fear of being caught, we stop stepping out of the house. I feel we should name our sufferings so that they all can sit separately and make it easier for us to understand which sadness accompanies which pain. And names like 'somebody else' make them sting a little less. It won't hurt as much if you call a pain somebody else's. If you call another 'insignificant', it will surely lose some of its worth. And if another pain is named 'mine', it would feel the love and maybe smile upon us.

She threw a stone at the windows and shattered their glass. She had resolved to break her dreams. She pushed the bed between the walls and the space in the windows. It was half inside and half hanging out. She wanted to see the dreams that had no connection with the past. What do the dreams of today look like? Dreams of right now? She lay down. She couldn't see the roof of good advice that she had received from her dear ones. She could only see the sky filled with stars. She closed her eyes. She had chalk and a duster in her hands. She wiped all the other dreams out and started drawing—a city that she had never seen, trees that had no names and people who talked to her without asking her name.

I have tried a lot. I wanted to be Phantom (from *The Story of the Phantom: The Ghost Who Walks*) all my childhood, even if it was just for a day. I wore my underwear over tight pants and showed up in front of my 'enemies'. But they laughed. I would try to convince them with my fighting but would get beaten up in the end. I always felt that I have a superpower. If I couldn't be Phantom, then maybe I could become invisible or fly or at least bend spoons with my eyes. But as I grew up, I realized that I could not do any of that. Then I started thinking that maybe I would meet someone with superpowers one day. Maybe one day I'll bump into Phantom! I will say, 'Please, Phantom, be my best friend.' But we never met.

Now even flying in aeroplanes bores me. Wherever I go, everyone can see me. I had bent the spoons as soon as I'd bought them.

Even after all of this, when I lie in bed at night, I hear the hooves of a white horse. The dog Sheru starts barking, and a ghost comes and whispers, 'Get up, Phantom', and I am happy again.

About the Translator

Nandini is a writer and translator from Dehradun, Uttarakhand. She has written two books in Hindi—*Baaki ki Baat* and *Neeli*, which won the Amazon Pen to Publish Award 2019. Be it her hometown of Dehradun or her new home in Montana (US), this new mother can be found writing or complaining about not having enough time to write. When she is not writing, she's cooking, hiking or changing diapers with her husband.